Gay Marriage

by Kevin Hillstrom

LUCENT BOOKS

A part of Gale, Cengage Learning

GALE
CENGAGE Learning·

Detroit • New York • San Francisco • New Haven, Conn • Waterville, Maine • London

GALE
CENGAGE Learning

LIBRARY OF CONGRESS CATALOGING-IN-PUBLICATION DATA

Hillstrom, Kevin, 1963-
  Gay marriage / by Kevin Hillstrom.
    pages cm. -- (Hot topics)
  Includes bibliographical references and index.
  ISBN 978-1-4205-0870-3 (hardcover)
  1. Same-sex marriage--United States--Juvenile literature. I. Title.
  HQ1034.U5H55 2014
  306.84'80973--dc23

                                              2013038458

Lucent Books
27500 Drake Rd.
Farmington Hills, MI 48331

ISBN-13: 978-1-4205-0870-3
ISBN-10: 1-4205-0870-9

Printed in the United States of America
1 2 3 4 5 6 7 18 17 16 15 14

CONTENTS

FOREWORD

Young people today are bombarded with information. Aside from traditional sources such as newspapers, television, and the radio, they are inundated with a nearly continuous stream of data from electronic media. They send and receive e-mails and instant messages, read and write online "blogs," participate in chat rooms and forums, and surf the web for hours. This trend is likely to continue. As Patricia Senn Breivik, the former dean of university libraries at Wayne State University in Detroit, has stated, "Information overload will only increase in the future. By 2020, for example, the available body of information is expected to double every 73 days! How will these students find the information they need in this coming tidal wave of information?"

Ironically, this overabundance of information can actually impede efforts to understand complex issues. Whether the topic is abortion, the death penalty, gay rights, or obesity, the deluge of fact and opinion that floods the print and electronic media is overwhelming. The news media report the results of polls and studies that contradict one another. Cable news shows, talk radio programs, and newspaper editorials promote narrow viewpoints and omit facts that challenge their own political biases. The World Wide Web is an electronic minefield where legitimate scholars compete with the postings of ordinary citizens who may or may not be well-informed or capable of reasoned argument. At times, strongly worded testimonials and opinion pieces both in print and electronic media are presented as factual accounts.

Conflicting quotes and statistics can confuse even the most diligent researchers. A good example of this is the question of whether or not the death penalty deters crime. For instance, one study found that murders decreased by nearly one-third when the death penalty was reinstated in New York in 1995. Death penalty supporters cite this finding to support their argument that the existence of the death penalty deters criminals from committing murder. However, another study found that states without the death penalty have murder rates below the national average. This study is cited by opponents of capital punishment, who reject the claim that the death penalty deters murder. Students need context and clear, informed discussion if they are to think critically and make informed decisions.

The Hot Topics series is designed to help young people wade through the glut of fact, opinion, and rhetoric so that they can think critically about controversial issues. Only by reading and thinking critically will they be able to formulate a viewpoint that is not simply the parroted views of others. Each volume of the series focuses on one of today's most pressing social issues and provides a balanced overview of the topic. Carefully crafted narrative, fully documented primary and secondary source quotes, informative sidebars, and study questions all provide excellent starting points for research and discussion. Full-color photographs and charts enhance all volumes in the series. With its many useful features, the Hot Topics series is a valuable resource for young people struggling to understand the pressing issues of the modern era.

INTRODUCTION

THE STRUGGLE OVER GAY MARRIAGE

Half a century ago, few Americans would have predicted that gay marriage would rank as one of the most controversial and high-profile social issues of the early twenty-first century. Back in the 1950s and 1960s, homosexuality was widely reviled as a sign of sickness and immorality. Most gay men and women hid their sexual orientation from their families, friends, neighbors, and bosses to avoid persecution or abandonment. This hiding would come to be known as staying "in the closet," and for many homosexuals it seemed to be the only option available to them.

This state of affairs changed, however. At first this change was almost imperceptible, but eventually it took on a speed and momentum that both homosexuals and heterosexuals—also known as straights—sometimes found disorienting. A 1969 riot between gays and police at a New York bar called Stonewall sparked the birth of a gay rights movement, and during the 1970s and 1980s gay men and lesbian women came out of the closet in growing numbers. During this same time, a deadly new disease—AIDS—swooped down out of nowhere to claim the lives of tens of thousands of gay men. This tragedy, however, also deepened the resolve of gay men and women to obtain the same legal rights and the same level of respect that America's heterosexual citizens enjoyed.

From the 1990s and into the first decade of the twenty-first century, gay Americans intensified their efforts to obtain equal rights—including the right to marry their same-sex partners. The crusade for gay rights experienced many setbacks during this era, however. Millions of Americans deeply disapprove of homosexuality on religious and moral grounds. Conservative lawmakers, media figures, and religious leaders all banded together to oppose what they called the "radical gay agenda." They were particularly determined to preserve marriage as an institution for opposite-sex couples, and they succeeded in passing a wide range of state laws banning gay marriage.

In recent years, however, momentum has shifted in the battle over gay marriage. Capitalizing on rising levels of public acceptance and political support, gay and straight supporters of same-sex marriage have been able to legalize gay marriage in a handful of states. Some activists now openly discuss the possibility of gay marriage spreading across the entire United States. Opponents of gay marriage, however, despair at this idea. They vow to continue their fight to keep same-sex marriage from "corrupting" America's culture and its traditional marriage structure.

A HISTORY OF GAY RIGHTS IN AMERICA

Homosexuals in the United States currently enjoy higher levels of acceptance and equality in American neighborhoods and workplaces than ever before. This is only a recent phenomenon, however. For decades homosexuals were forced to remain "in the closet," keeping their sexual orientation carefully hidden in order to avoid blatant discrimination and the threat of violent physical attacks. Many homosexuals "came out" during the gay rights movement of the 1970s to win important legal and social victories, only to face a conservative backlash during the AIDS crisis of the 1980s. The turn of the twenty-first century marked the beginning of a new era in the fight for lesbian, gay, bisexual, and transgendered (LGBT) rights, with activists shifting their focus toward gaining access to one of the nation's most cherished cultural and religious institutions: marriage.

Homosexuality Through History

Homosexuality—romantic love or sexual attraction that is directed toward a person of the same sex—has existed since the beginning of human history. The ancient Greek philosopher Plato wrote approvingly about same-sex relationships in such influential texts as the *Symposium*. Same-sex relationships were common and generally accepted in many early Native American cultures as well.

Although some cultures viewed homosexual relations as a natural expression of human sexuality, many religious traditions considered it a sin. The Bible contains several passages that appear to condemn homosexuality, including Leviticus 18:22, which warns "Thou shalt not lie with mankind, as with woman-

kind: it is abomination." Conservative Christians have interpret-
ed such passages to mean that same-sex relationships contradict
God's will and must be prohibited.

European colonists carried this view of homosexuality—as
something abnormal and immoral—with them to the New World.
The American colonies enacted harsh punishments for homosexual behavior, including death by hanging. Homosexuality continued to be widely condemned through the 1800s, but in the early
1900s, homosexual-friendly communities formed in many rap-
idly growing urban areas. These enclaves—in New York City, Los
Angeles, San Francisco, and other cities—brought greater public
visibility to same-sex romantic relationships. As a result, homosexuality became an area of study for psychiatrists and other health
professionals. In 1910 the pioneering psychoanalyst Sigmund
Freud described homosexuality as one of several common "deviations" in human sexual function. He attributed "inverted" sexual

*Capitalizing on rising levels of public acceptance and political support, gay and
straight supporters of same-sex marriage have been able to get same-sex marriage
legalized in a handful of states.*

In 1910 the father of modern psychoanalysis, Sigmund Freud, described homosexuality as one of several common "deviations" in human psychosexual development.

orientation to a combination of biological and psychological influences. Freud decided that most homosexuals could not be "cured" through psychoanalysis or other forms of medical treatment, so he counseled people to accept them in society.

Homosexuals Face Hostility and Discrimination

While Freud and other researchers sought to understand homosexuality, most Americans held hostile attitudes toward same-sex relationships—especially in the socially conservative era following World War II. Homosexuality continued to be viewed as unnatural and immoral, and suspected homosexuals endured insults, humiliation, harassment, threats, and violence from classmates, coworkers, and even law enforcement officials. They were also accused of being perverts, sex maniacs, and child molesters. As a result, many homosexuals chose to remain "in the closet," keeping their sexual orientation hidden.

Homosexuals had even more reason to stay closeted as the U.S. government and many state governments enacted laws and policies that discriminated against homosexuals and criminalized same-sex relationships. So-called sodomy laws existed in every state until 1962, when Illinois became the first state to repeal them. These laws prohibited various sexual acts including those typical of homosexual relationships. Although sodomy laws in many states were written broadly enough to apply to heterosexual relations, enforcement of the laws usually targeted homosexuals.

Writer James Baldwin Defends Homosexuality

"Everybody's journey is individual. If you fall in love with a boy, you fall in love with a boy. The fact that many Americans consider it a disease says more about them than it does about homosexuality."—writer James Baldwin

Quoted in Dawn Marie Daniels and Candace Sandy. *Souls of My Brothers.* New York: Plume, 2003, p. 246.

Throughout the 1950s and 1960s, law enforcement officials kept track of suspected homosexuals and watched over the places where they gathered. Police in many cities conducted frequent raids of bars and nightclubs that catered to homosexuals. Patrons of these establishments were often subjected to police brutality, including beatings, sexual assaults, and indefinite detainments. In some cases law enforcement officials would reveal the names of people caught up in the raids to local newspapers.

Discrimination in employment was another serious problem for homosexuals in the mid-twentieth century. In 1950 the U.S. Senate issued a report titled "Employment of Homosexuals and Other Sex Perverts in Government," which argued that homosexuals should be prohibited from working for the federal government. "Homosexuals and other sex perverts are not proper persons to be employed in Government for two reasons; first, they are generally unsuitable, and second, they constitute security risks," the report stated. "Those who engage in overt acts of perversion lack the emotional stability of normal persons."[1]

President Dwight Eisenhower adopted the recommendations of the Senate report in 1953, when he signed Executive Order 10450. This order claimed that homosexuals—along with alco-

In 1953 President Dwight D. Eisenhower signed Executive Order 10450. This order claimed that homosexuals—along with alcoholics, drug addicts, and people with psychological disorders—posed a national security risk if given government or military positions.

holics, drug addicts, and people with psychological disorders—posed a risk to national security. Eisenhower thus banned them from working for the federal government or its private contractors. His order resulted in the dismissal of around five hundred alleged homosexuals from federal government jobs and the expulsion of more than forty-three hundred men from the U.S. military. Homosexuals were routinely denied employment in the public sector or removed from jobs in government agencies until the order was revoked by President Richard Nixon in 1974. Nixon's order did not apply to the armed forces, though, and homosexuals were not allowed to serve openly in the U.S. military until 2011.

Executive Order 10450 also sent a clear antigay message to privately owned businesses. Many private employers thus followed the federal government's lead and either refused to hire openly homosexual employees or fired those who came out of the closet or who were even suspected of being homosexual.

The Medical Community Weighs In

The U.S. government based some of its policies regarding the employment of homosexuals on judgments of the medical community. In 1952 the American Psychiatric Association published the first edition of its *Diagnostic and Statistical Manual of Mental Disorders*. Aimed at doctors and medical researchers, the manual provided guidelines to aid in the diagnosis and treatment of various psychiatric conditions. It listed homosexuality as a type of mental illness known as sociopathic personality disturbance.

This finding conflicted with the results of studies conducted by various medical professionals around that time. The prominent biologist and sex researcher Alfred Kinsey, for example, published his influential book *Sexual Behavior in the Human Male* in 1948. Kinsey reported that 37 percent of the men he interviewed had participated in homosexual activities at least one time. Since many of these men eventually established long-term heterosexual relationships, Kinsey concluded that same-sex experimentation was fairly common and was not restricted to people who identified themselves as homosexual. The American psychologist Evelyn Hooker also challenged the idea that homosexuality was a mental disorder in the 1950s. Despite the work of Kinsey, Hooker, and other experts, however, the American Psychiatric Association did not change its classification of homosexuality as a disorder until 1973.

Homosexuals Seek Equal Rights

The first organized efforts to increase public acceptance and understanding of homosexuality occurred in the 1950s. Activist Harry Hay founded the first national homosexual rights organization, called the Mattachine Society, in Los Angeles in 1950. In 1953 several Mattachine members began publishing *One: The Homosexual Magazine,* the first news and culture periodical intended for homosexual readers in U.S. history. The first national organization for female homosexuals, the Daughters of Bilitis (DOB), was founded in San Francisco in 1955. By the early 1960s, the DOB had expanded to include chapters in New York, Chicago, and other major cities. Members also launched an influential magazine called the *Ladder.*

Homophobia and Hate Crimes

The word *homophobia* is used to describe extreme feelings of fear, hatred, and intolerance toward homosexuals. Psychologist George Weinberg coined the term in his 1972 book *Society and the Healthy Homosexual.* A 2000 study by the Kaiser Family Foundation, for instance, found that 75 percent of lesbian, gay, bisexual, transgender (LGBT) individuals had been the targets of verbal abuse or harassment from homophobic Americans, and that 33 percent had been the victims of physical violence because of their sexual orientation.

Acceptance of gays in American society has increased in recent years, but homophobic violence and harassment is still a problem. "The more visible you are as a community the more vulnerable you are, too," said Suzanna Walters, a professor of gender studies. "There is a protection in the closet, as awful as that is. Real homophobia with violent outcomes is not a thing of the past and there is much more work to be done."

Quoted in Natalie DiBlasio. "Crimes Against LGBT Community Are Up, Despite Social Gains." *USA Today,* August 1, 2011. http://usatoday30.usatoday.com/news /nation/2011-07-31-LGBT-violence-lesbian-gay-trans gender-bisexual-survey_n.htm.

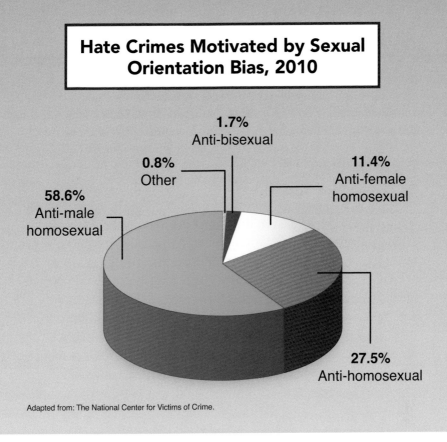

Hate Crimes Motivated by Sexual Orientation Bias, 2010

1.7%
Anti-bisexual

0.8%
Other

11.4%
Anti-female
homosexual

58.6%
Anti-male
homosexual

27.5%
Anti-homosexual

Adapted from: The National Center for Victims of Crime.

Advocates of homosexual rights scored an important legal victory in 1958, after the U.S. Postal Service refused to deliver *One* on the grounds that its content was obscene. In the landmark case *One, Inc. v. Olesen,* the United States Supreme Court ruled that *One* was protected under the First Amendment of the Constitution, which guarantees American citizens the right to freedom of speech and freedom of the press. The decision marked the first time that the Supreme Court ruled in favor of homosexual rights.

A New Era of Civil Rights Activism

The movement for homosexual rights gained momentum during the 1960s. It was a decade of protest marches, demonstrations, and social turmoil as African Americans and other minority groups fought to end discrimination and achieve equality in American society. Their efforts resulted in landmark legislation like the Civil Rights Act of 1964, which outlawed discrimination on the basis of race, color, religion, sex, or national origin in employment, education, and public accommodations.

These movements encouraged homosexuals to assert their rights as well. Frank Kameny emerged as a prominent figure in these early efforts to end discrimination against homosexuals. Kameny worked as an astronomer for the U.S. Army's map service until he was fired from his job and barred from government employment because of his homosexuality. He responded by filing a lawsuit and pursuing appeals all the way to the U.S. Supreme Court. Although the Court declined to hear the case in 1961, Kameny's outspoken activism helped bring a more militant tone to the campaign for homosexual civil rights.

During the late 1960s New York City became the staging ground for a homosexual rights movement that eventually spread across the country. New York City was home to the largest homosexual population in the United States at that time, despite the fact that city leaders were actively hostile to their presence. The New York Police Department, for instance, established spe-

In the 1960s Frank Kameny was a prominent figure in early efforts to end discrimination against homosexuals.

cial vice squads to uphold sodomy laws. City law enforcement officers also raided bars and bath houses that were frequented by homosexuals.

The city's crackdown on homosexual activity created a great deal of tension between police and New York's homosexual population. "It was a nightmare for the lesbian or gay man who was arrested and caught up in the juggernaut, but it was also a nightmare for the lesbians or gay men who lived in the closet," Yale Law School professor William Eskridge explained in the PBS film *Stonewall Uprising*. "This produced an enormous amount of anger within the lesbian and gay community in New York City. Eventually something was bound to blow."[2]

The Stonewall Uprising

The explosive event that is widely viewed as the start of the gay rights movement occurred on June 28, 1969. Late that night, New York police officers raided the Stonewall Inn, a well-known bar on Christopher Street in Greenwich Village that catered to homosexuals. Although the police claimed to be investigating liquor law violations, the bar's patrons viewed the raid as part of an ongoing campaign of harassment and intimidation by city authorities.

On that evening, the bar's patrons decided that they were fed up. People inside the bar refused to leave and resisted arrest. People outside the establishment threw rocks and bottles at police. The confrontation lasted for several more nights, as a crowd of up to two thousand homosexuals and their straight allies gathered in protest at the Stonewall Inn. The protesters—many of them dressed in flamboyant outfits—chanted, held up signs, and refused to follow police orders to disperse.

The Stonewall uprising, as the incident came to be known, marked the first time that the homosexual community had taken a united stand against discriminatory treatment. It also inspired many homosexuals across the country to speak out and demand equality for the first time. "Before Stonewall, I could never see gay people coming together and organizing or marching down the street for any kind of protest," activist John O'Brien said in PBS's *Stonewall Uprising*. "The many people inspired by Stonewall who then became involved in the GLBT [gay, lesbian, bisexual, and transgender] movement directly changed the horrible conditions and status of gay and lesbians, replacing fear with pride."[3]

The Gay Rights Movement

Within a year of the Stonewall uprising, members of the LGBT community and their straight allies formed as many as one thousand new organizations to continue the push for equal rights. Many of these organizations adopted the term "gay" in their names, including the Gay Liberation Front and the Gay Activists' Alliance. Gay originally meant "carefree," and during the 1800s this meaning grew to encompass uninhibited sexual behavior. It was not applied specifically to homosexuals until the mid-twentieth century, and even then it was usually intended as a derogatory term. By appropriating the term for their own use, gay activists expressed pride in their identity.

The growing strength and size of the gay rights movement became clear in 1970, when more than five thousand people marched from Greenwich Village to Central Park in New York City to commemorate the first anniversary of the Stonewall uprising. This event, which became known locally as Christopher Street Liberation Day, is widely considered to be the first gay pride parade held in the United States. Recognition of the anniversary expanded in subsequent years, as Stonewall became enshrined as the historic birthplace of the LGBT rights movement.

LGBT activists became increasingly open and defiant during the 1970s. The gay rights movement initiated a "coming out" strategy during this time, in which gay and lesbian individuals were encouraged to publicly disclose their homosexuality. Activists also formed support groups to allow people to share their experiences and feel less isolated. As more and more people came out of the closet and acknowledged their sexuality to family, friends, coworkers, and employers, the LGBT rights movement grew more visible and gained strength as a political force.

One of the pioneering gay voices in politics belonged to Harvey Milk, who won a seat on the city of San Francisco's Board of Supervisors in 1977. Shortly after his election, Milk introduced a gay rights ordinance designed to protect the city's LGBT

The Rainbow Flag

The rainbow flag emerged as a symbol of gay pride during the gay rights movement of the 1970s. San Francisco artist Gilbert Baker created the original rainbow flag in 1978 for the city's Gay Freedom Day parade. It featured eight horizontal stripes in different colors: hot pink, red, orange, yellow, green, turquoise, indigo, and violet. Within a year the hot pink and turquoise stripes were eliminated and the indigo stripe was changed to royal blue. The rainbow colors represent the diversity of the gay rights movement.

In 2003, in honor of the flag's twenty-fifth anniversary, Baker created the world's largest rainbow flag. It was 1.25 miles (2.0km) long and required two thousand volunteers to unfurl it across the span of Key West, Florida. Afterward, the flag was cut into strips that were displayed at gay rights events in more than one hundred cities around the world.

The rainbow flag emerged as the symbol of gay pride during the gay liberation movement of the 1970s.

residents from employment discrimination. He also led a successful campaign to defeat Proposition 6, a 1978 California ballot initiative that would have banned gays and lesbians—as well as heterosexuals who supported gay rights—from teaching in public schools.

A VIOLATION OF GOD'S LAWS

"Any sex outside of the marriage bond between a man and a woman is violating God's law. So obviously the homosexual is immediately violating God's laws. It is not a sin to have latent desire or to be tempted immorally. The sin is when you yield to the temptation."—Southern Baptist pastor and televangelist Jerry Falwell

Quoted in "Interview: Reverend Jerry Falwell." *Frontline*: Assault on Gay America, PBS, 2000. www.pbs.org/wgbh/pages/frontline/shows/assault/interviews/falwell.html.

LGBT activists took their campaign for equal rights to the nation's capital in 1979. On October 14 of that year, an estimated seventy-five thousand people participated in the March on Washington for Lesbian and Gay Rights. The march caught the attention of the Democratic Party, which became the first national political party to adopt a homosexual rights platform at its 1980 convention. Two years later, Wisconsin became the first state to ban discrimination on the basis of sexual orientation.

Conservative Backlash and the AIDS Crisis

The political gains of the LGBT rights movement during the late 1970s and early 1980s prompted an antigay backlash from social conservatives. One of the most prominent critics of homosexuality during this time was Anita Bryant, a popular singer, former Miss America beauty pageant contestant, and commercial spokesperson for Florida orange juice and other products. As a Southern Baptist, Bryant considered homosexuality a sin, and she claimed that LGBT individuals threatened to corrupt the morality of children. "As a mother, I know that homosexuals cannot biologically reproduce children," she declared. "Therefore, they must recruit our children."[4]

In 1977 Dade County, Florida, passed an ordinance prohibiting discrimination on the basis of sexual orientation. Bryant mobilized opposition to the measure under the banner "Save Our Children." With vocal support from such nationally known figures as the Reverend Jerry Falwell, her campaign succeeded in repealing the antidiscrimination ordinance. Bryant's outspoken opposition to gay rights made her a highly controversial figure, however. Gay rights supporters retaliated by signing petitions, attending rallies, and organizing a boycott of Florida orange juice and other products she endorsed. The controversy effectively ended Bryant's career, but Dade County did not reinstate gay rights protections for twenty years.

The cause of homosexual equality suffered another blow in 1981, when the American medical community reported the first cases of extremely rare lung infections, skin lesions, and cancers among gay men. These illnesses appeared to be caused by deficiencies in the patients' immune systems, which rendered them incapable of fighting off germs that did not harm healthy people. Since the mysterious disease disproportionately affected gay men, and homosexual relations seemed to be involved in its transmission, doctors initially called it Gay-Related Immune Deficiency (GRID). Before long, though, the same symptoms began appearing in heterosexuals from other demographic groups, such as Haitian immigrants, people who received blood transfusions, and intravenous drug users. The disease was renamed Acquired Immune Deficiency Syndrome (AIDS), and in 1986 scientists identified the virus that caused it as the human immunodeficiency virus (HIV).

AIDS Galvanizes New Activism

The U.S. government was slow to respond to the AIDS crisis. Margaret Heckler, a former congresswoman with no public-health experience, became the point person for the federal response when she took over as President Ronald Reagan's secretary of health and human services in 1983. Heckler attempted to reassure the public by repeatedly claiming that the nation's blood supply was "100 percent safe," and she came under intense criticism when this statement turned out to be incorrect. Reagan himself remained silent on the subject of AIDS until 1987, when he addressed the Third International Conference on AIDS in Washington, D.C. By that time more than thirty-six thousand Americans had been diagnosed with the disease, and nearly twenty-one thousand had died from it. Critics argued that earlier and more decisive action by the Reagan administration might have prevented AIDS from becoming a worldwide pandemic.

In the absence of medical knowledge about the transmission of HIV and the factors that put people at risk, many Americans grappled with making sense of this new threat. Some conservative religious leaders claimed that immorality and sexual promiscuity on the part of homosexuals was responsible for the AIDS crisis. Falwell, for example, expressed the opinion that "AIDS is the wrath of God upon homosexuals."[5] As AIDS fears gripped the nation, many Americans blamed homosexuals for bringing this new public health threat to the nation's doorstep. Journalist Eric Marcus also noted that the disease "forced celebrities and tens of thousands of other gay men out of the closet and into the public eye."[6]

This tension-filled atmosphere spurred gay rights activists back into action. In 1983 author Larry Kramer issued an urgent warning to the gay community about the AIDS crisis in an article for the *New York Native,* a gay weekly newspaper. "If this article doesn't rouse you to anger, fury, rage, and action, gay men may have no future on this earth," he wrote. "Our continued existence depends on just how angry you can get."[7] Kramer went on to found AIDS Coalition to Unleash Power (ACT UP), the first AIDS advocacy group. In 1987 ACT UP organized a Gay March on Washington that attracted an estimated five hundred thousand people. Marchers urged the federal government to increase funding for AIDS research and treatment, end discrimination against homosexuals, repeal sodomy laws, and provide legal recognition for lesbian and gay relationships.

The massive gay rights protest in the nation's capital marked a turning point in the fight against AIDS. In 1988 U.S. surgeon general C. Everett Koop sent an eight-page booklet called *Un-*

Jerry Falwell led the conservative mantra that said, "AIDS is the wrath of God upon homosexuals."

derstanding AIDS to over 100 million households across the country. It was the first time that federal authorities provided the American people with clear medical information about the disease and the most effective means of protecting against its spread. In 1990 President George H.W. Bush signed the Ryan White Care Act into law. The act, named after a young man who contracted HIV through a blood transfusion for hemophilia, provided massive funding increases for AIDS research and support programs. These programs led to the development of anti-retroviral drugs that slow the progression of HIV in many patients, allowing them to live for years or even decades without developing AIDS.

Barriers Begin to Fall

As LGBT activists achieved successes in the fight against AIDS, they also made gains in the fight to end discrimination on the basis of sexual orientation or identity. In 1993 the U.S. Department of Defense lifted its ban on homosexuals serving in the military—although it still prohibited them from serving openly. Under the new policy, military recruiters were not allowed to ask applicants about their sexual orientation. In addition, gay and lesbian service members were not allowed to reveal their homosexuality or engage in homosexual acts. The policy thus became known as "Don't Ask, Don't Tell" (DADT).

The DADT policy was controversial from the beginning. Conservatives still did not like the idea of gays—even closeted ones—serving in the military. Critics on the left, meanwhile, said that it was unfair for soldiers who risked their lives for their country to have to hide their sexual orientation. By 2010 DADT had resulted in the discharge of 13,650 service members for disclosing their homosexuality or engaging in homosexual activities. This loss of trained military personnel, and the resulting need to recruit and train replacements, cost American taxpayers an estimated $400 million. Congress repealed DADT in late 2010, and in 2011 homosexuals were allowed to serve openly in the U.S. military for the first time.

Gay rights activists earned another victory in 1996, when the U.S. Supreme Court issued its ruling in *Romer v. Evans*. The case concerned a Colorado constitutional amendment that prohibited local governments from adopting statutes that gave special protection to homosexuals. The Court invalidated the amendment, declaring that the state could not offer protection against discrimination to some of its citizens and deny those same safeguards to homosexuals.

In 2003 the Court decided that state sodomy laws were unconstitutional in *Lawrence v. Texas*. Justice Anthony Kennedy wrote that "the statutes seek to control a personal relationship that is within the liberty of persons to choose without being punished as criminals."[8] Gay rights advocates celebrated the ruling, which essentially made homosexual activity legal across the country.

Homosexuals received new federal civil rights protections in 2009, when Congress passed the Matthew Shepard Act. Shepard was a gay twenty-one-year-old student at the University of Wyoming who was beaten, tortured, and left tied to a fence to die in 1998. Prosecutors claimed that the two men responsible murdered Shepard because of his sexual orientation. The act expanded U.S. hate crime laws to cover crimes motivated by a victim's actual or perceived gender, sexual orientation, gender identity, or disability.

MARRIAGE—THE FINAL FRONTIER IN GAY RIGHTS

During the early years of the gay rights movement, the right to marry one's same-sex partner was not a big priority. Over time, however, gays and lesbians changed their perspective. They came to see marriage as the final frontier in their quest for full equality with straight family members, friends, and neighbors. The subsequent push to legalize same-sex marriage aroused fierce opposition, though. During the 1990s and 2000s, a great wall of legislation designed to protect traditional, opposite-sex marriage and forbid same-sex unions was erected by both federal and state lawmakers. In 2012, however, gay marriage advocates celebrated a series of major triumphs and milestones that advanced their cause.

Changing Attitudes Within the Gay Community

As the gay rights movement gained momentum in the 1970s and 1980s, relatively few activists concerned themselves with the issue of marriage. Many gay Americans saw marriage as an institution that oppressed the sexuality of men and women, stifled their individuality, and forced them to conform to mainstream culture. They wanted instead to push the United States toward greater acceptance of gay culture and lifestyle choices.

As time passed, however, many gays and lesbians reassessed their stances of indifference or hostility to marriage. Some gays—and especially those raising children from adoption or previous heterosexual relationships—expressed a desire for the stability and safety that can be found in married households. In addition, gays came to recognize that marriage—and legal parallels to marriage like so-called civil unions or domestic partnerships—offers legal rights that are not available to unmarried couples. These benefits include child custody, support, and adoption rights; inheritance and ownership rights; access to insurance, pensions, and tax benefits; and increased authority to make medical decisions for loved ones.

As calls for "marriage equality" grew in strength, millions of Americans lined up in opposition. Critics of gay marriage cited religious beliefs about the sinfulness of homosexuality and fears about the impact of same-sex marriage on American culture and traditional, opposite-sex marriage. Undaunted, advocates of gay marriage and civil unions pointed out that the institution of marriage had already undergone other changes over the last one hundred years, such as the right to use birth control or marry people of other races. "Viewed from the distance of time, we can see that society was not harmed by these changes, despite the discomfort,

Discrimination experienced by many gays during the AIDS crisis in the late 1980s spurred greater militancy among gay activists, and committed but legally unmarried gay couples began demanding benefits enjoyed by heterosexual couples.

scare tactics, and threats at the time," wrote gay marriage advocate Evan Wolfson. "Quite to the contrary, society is, in fact, stronger because of these changes."[9]

Early Advances and Setbacks

The early fight to legalize same-sex marriage was shaped by several influential Supreme Court rulings of the 1960s, 1970s, and 1980s. Gay marriage activists compared laws forbidding same-sex unions to bans on interracial marriage, which had been struck down as unconstitutional by the U.S. Supreme Court in the 1967 case *Loving v. Virginia*. Activists also realized that they would have to pursue gay marriage on a state-by-state basis due to the 1972 Supreme Court decision *Baker v. Nelson*. According to this ruling, gay marriage was not an issue for the federal government to decide.

Advocates of gay marriage also realized that another Supreme Court ruling—*Bowers v. Hardwick*—posed a major hurdle to their cause. This 1986 decision upheld a law in the state of Georgia that banned sodomy (generally understood to be any type of sexual penetration other than penile-vaginal intercourse between heterosexual couples). The Court found no constitutional protection for acts of sodomy, and it ruled that states had the right to outlaw such practices. Since all sexual activity between gay and lesbian couples is by definition sodomy, the *Bowers v. Hardwick* decision was a serious blow to the gay marriage cause.

In other areas, though, gay men and women made inroads into sectors of American life that had previously been closed to them. "During the 1980s, more than fifty openly gay and lesbian people were elected and reelected to public office," observed journalist Eric Marcus.

> The first openly gay and lesbian judges were appointed to the bench. . . . Several [religious denominations] ordained openly lesbian and gay clergy. And an increasing number of religious leaders expressed support for the blessing of same-gender relationships. By the start of the 1990s, more than 100 cities and counties and four states had passed laws protecting the rights of gay people, and several municipalities passed domestic-partnership laws that extended limited, but symbolically important, rights to same-gender couples.[10]

Hawaii Case Spurs the Passage of DOMA

In the early 1990s the debate over gay marriage abruptly exploded into the national consciousness. Prior to this time, gay marriage had not attracted broad popular notice. The only people who seemed to care about the issue were a small contingent of dedicated gay activists and a modest number of equally dedicated conservative opponents. In 1993, however, the Hawaii Supreme Court agreed to consider the case of three gay couples who wanted to marry, despite a state ban on same-sex marriage. "To everyone's astonishment," wrote gay historian and activist George Chauncey, "the Hawaii plaintiffs came within an inch of winning full marriage rights."[11] The justices determined that the same-sex marriage ban violated the state's constitutional guarantee of equal rights. They sent the case (known originally as *Baehr v. Lewin* and later as *Baehr v. Miike*) back to a lower court with instructions to determine whether there was any "compelling" reason to sanction such discrimination.

This event mobilized both foes and supporters of same-sex marriage. Conservative religious organizations redirected their significant financial, legal, and public relations resources at gay marriage, which they saw as an emerging threat to traditional family structures and national morality. But the Hawaii case also

Civil Unions and Domestic Partnerships

Civil unions are legal arrangements that grant same-sex couples most of the rights of state-approved civil marriages, including spousal support, medical decision-making privileges, coverage on a partner's insurance, and hospital visitation rights. They do not have the sacred or traditional aspects of a religious or church-sanctioned marriage, however, and they do not provide federal benefits of marriage, such as Social Security benefits. Domestic partnerships, which can also be entered into by unmarried straight couples, are similar to civil unions in many respects. The rights and responsibilities contained in domestic partnerships, however, vary widely from state to state.

"unleashed a tremendous energy amongst gay and non-gay people on our side,"[12] recalled Wolfson.

For the next several years, the battle over same-sex marriage was a rout. Opponents of gay marriage took advantage of public discomfort with legalizing same-sex unions to register a series of important legal and political victories. Conservatives hailing from the worlds of politics, religion, and media applauded as numerous states passed new laws and constitutional amendments to legally reserve marriage for opposite-sex couples.

A CALL FOR RESTORATION OF TRADITIONAL MARRIAGE

"In these days when [traditional, opposite-sex] marriage has already been weakened by many social forces, what is needed is restoration and revitalization of marriage, not a mutation of it to erase what remains of its institutional integrity."—Law professor Lynn D. Wardle

Lynn D. Wardle. "Beyond Equality." In *Marriage and Same-Sex Unions: A Debate*, edited by Lynn D. Wardle et al.. Westport, CT: Praeger, 2003, p. 188.

These laws and amendments eventually came to be known as "mini-DOMAs," after the federal Defense of Marriage Act (DOMA). This federal legislation was passed by Congress in 1996 with strong support from both Republicans and Democrats. DOMA passed in the House of Representatives by a 342–67 vote and sailed through the Senate by an 85–14 vote. It was then formally signed into law by Democratic president Bill Clinton. The Defense of Marriage Act constituted a crushing blow to gay marriage crusaders. It explicitly defined marriage as a union between a man and a woman. It thus forbade gay and lesbian couples from receiving legal and financial benefits traditionally conferred by marriage in such areas as Social Security benefits, federal income taxes, and federal estate taxes. DOMA also stipulated that states were not required to recognize same-sex marriages from other states.

Even Hawaii brought bad news for gay marriage advocates during this period. In 1998 Hawaii voters approved a constitutional amendment outlawing same-sex marriage. This revision to the state constitution meant that the Hawaii Supreme Court could no longer strike down gay marriage bans as unconstitutional.

Landmark Legislation in Vermont

These legal and political setbacks discouraged supporters of gay marriage but did not stop them from continuing the fight. Gay activists and their supporters in the straight community continued to make the case for full marriage equality. "We want full integration into civil institutions, the same rules, the same principles of responsibility," said Andrew Sullivan, one of the most visible and outspoken advocates for same-sex marriage. "The antigay marriage forces have—what exactly? They are against civil unions, against domestic partnerships, against military service, against any form of recognition. They want to create a shadow class of people operating somehow in a cultural and social limbo.

Stan Baker, left, was one of three plaintiffs that brought their discrimination suit before the Vermont Supreme Court in the late 1990s. In December 1999 the high court ruled that the state had a constitutional obligation to grant same-sex couples the same legal benefits, protections, and responsibilities as married couples.

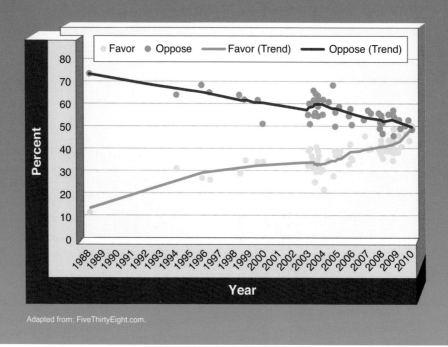

Same-Sex Marriage: U.S. Public Polls Since 1988

Adapted from: FiveThirtyEight.com.

That strategy may have worked as long as gay people cooperated—by staying in the closet, keeping their heads down. . . . But the cooperation is over."[13]

Efforts to generate support for same-sex marriage were aided by increasingly positive and sympathetic portrayals of gay people in American movies, television programs, and other popular media. Gay marriage advocates also benefited from the increased visibility of openly gay men and women in many American communities. These men and women recognized that living "out of the closet" was not as dangerous or isolating as it had been even a few decades earlier. Gay and lesbian couples thus became more commonplace, especially in so-called "blue" states—states with a high percentage of liberal or Democratic residents (conservative Republican states, by contrast, have come to be known as "red" states).

In 1999 the campaign for marriage equality registered its first major victory. In December of that year, the Vermont Supreme Court ruled that the state had a constitutional obligation to grant same-sex couples the same legal benefits, protections, and responsibilities as married opposite-sex couples. State lawmakers responded in April 2000 by approving landmark legislation that officially recognized the legitimacy of civil unions between same-sex couples. The controversial new law, however, still preserved the term *marriage* for legally recognized unions of "one man and one woman."

Gay Marriage in Massachusetts and San Francisco

Three years later, legal challenges filed by advocates for gay rights resulted in another momentous victory. In November 2003 the Massachusetts Supreme Judicial Court ruled in *Goodridge v. Department of Public Health* that barring same-sex couples from civil marriage violated the state constitution. "The Massachusetts Constitution affirms the dignity and equality of all individuals," explained chief justice Margaret Marshall in the majority decision. "It forbids the creation of second-class citizens. In reaching our

In the Massachusetts Supreme Court's majority opinion in Goodrich v. Department of Public Health, *chief justice Margaret Marshall wrote that the state's constitution forbade the "creation of second-class citizens" and that Massachusetts had "failed to identify any constitutionally adequate reason for denying civil marriage to same-sex couples."*

conclusion we have given full deference to the arguments made by the Commonwealth. But it has failed to identify any constitutionally adequate reason for denying civil marriage to same-sex couples."[14]

Three months later, the Massachusetts Supreme Judicial Court added that "separate but equal" civil unions for gays would not be good enough; the state needed to let same-sex couples obtain the same marriage licenses that were available to opposite-sex couples. The state government obeyed this directive, and in May 2004 Massachusetts became the first state in the union to issue marriage licenses to same-sex couples—and to challenge the constitutionality of DOMA.

Meanwhile, Democratic mayor Gavin Newsom of San Francisco, California, announced on February 12, 2004, that the city intended to issue marriage licenses to same-sex couples, even though doing so would violate California laws. Approximately four thousand licenses were issued to gay and lesbian couples over the next month, but on March 11 the state Supreme Court halted this action. Five months later, the Court annulled the licenses, ruling that Newsom had acted without the necessary legal authority.

Conservative Republicans condemned Newsom for his actions, which they said reflected the gay rights movement's radical agenda (even though Newsom is straight). Fellow Democrats, meanwhile, were slow to come to his defense. "That whole issue [of gay marriage] has been too much, too fast, too soon," said Democratic senator Dianne Feinstein of California in late 2004. "People aren't ready for it."[15]

The Battle over Gay Marriage Heats Up

Gay marriage advocates were thrilled with the advent of gay marriage in Massachusetts, and they appreciated Newsom's efforts. They also celebrated *Lawrence v. Texas*, a June 2003 ruling by the U.S. Supreme Court that struck down all state sodomy laws as unconstitutional.

Conservative opponents of gay marriage, on the other hand, expressed grave concern about these developments, and they redoubled their efforts to stop same-sex marriage from spreading any further. "A man and a woman joined together in holy

On February 24, 2004, President George W. Bush publicly called for passage of an amendment to the U.S. Constitution that would define marriage as the "legal union between one man and one woman as husband and wife."

matrimony is the time-tested 'yardstick' for marriage," stated the Family Research Council. "One cannot alter the definition of marriage without throwing society into confusion any more than one can change the definition of a yardstick. Homosexual marriage is an empty pretense that lacks the fundamental sexual complementariness of male and female. And like all counterfeits, it cheapens and degrades the real thing."[16]

Critics of same-sex marriage found an ally in President George W. Bush. On February 24, 2004, Bush publicly called for passage of an amendment to the U.S. Constitution that would define marriage as the "legal union between one man and one woman as husband and wife." "The union of a man and a woman is the most enduring human institution, honored and encouraged in all cultures and by every religious faith," said Bush. "Ages of experience have taught humanity that the commitment of a husband and wife to love and to serve one another promotes the welfare of children and the stability of society. Marriage cannot be severed from its cultural, religious, and natural roots without weakening the good influence of society."[17]

A subsequent bill containing the proposed constitutional amendment to ban same-sex marriage failed to pass the U.S. Senate, to the great relief of gay activists. However, the 2004 and 2006 elections brought an avalanche of state-level referendums that made gay marriage illegal. In November 2004 eleven states passed constitutional amendments defining marriage as exclusively an opposite-sex institution. Two years later, constitutional amendments banning same-sex marriage passed in seven more states (Arizona voters rejected a similar measure on their ballot).

Triumphs and Setbacks for Both Sides

The next several years brought both joy and heartache to opponents of same-sex marriage. Defenders of traditional marriage celebrated in 2008, for example, when California voters approved Proposition 8, which banned gay marriage in the state. But they were deeply disappointed in April 2009, when Iowa began performing same-sex marriages after the state's supreme court struck down a gay marriage ban as unconstitutional.

REFUSING TO TAKE THE COMPLIMENT

"You would think that after spending three decades arguing that the Gay Lifestyle was a threat to the traditional family because it was so appealingly hedonistic . . . social conservatives would be delighted when huge numbers of gays and lesbians decided to embrace the Straight Lifestyle and marry. What a victory for traditional family values! . . . [But] social conservatives refuse to take the compliment. Gay people who want to settle down and live like straights are not an affirmation of the Straight Lifestyle, they insist, just another attack on it."—Gay rights advocate and writer Dan Savage

Dan Savage. *The Commitment: Love, Sex, Marriage, and My Family.* New York: Dutton, 2005, p. 149.

These same dramatic swings in emotion afflicted gay activists and their allies in the straight community. They applauded in 2007, when both New Jersey and New Hampshire began recognizing civil unions, and in 2008, when Connecticut legalized gay marriage. They also cheered in April 2009, when state legislators in Vermont overrode a veto by Republican governor Jim Douglas to pass a bill making Vermont the fourth state (behind Massachusetts, Connecticut, and Iowa) to legalize same-sex marriage. The legislature thus made Vermont the first state in the country to pass a statute allowing same-sex marriage without being forced to do so by the courts. But gay marriage advocates experienced disappointments, too, such as the November 2009 vote by the people of Maine to repeal a law that would have permitted gay marriage in the state.

Meanwhile, court battles continued to rage over DOMA, Proposition 8, and other laws and proposals designed to expand or limit the definition of marriage at state and federal levels. Most Republicans continued to oppose same-sex marriages and civil unions, and they continued to press for a constitutional amendment banning gay marriage. Pro–gay marriage activists, though, were heartened by growing support from Democrats in Congress and Democratic president Barack Obama, who in December 2010 said that he favored "a strong civil union that provides [gay couples] the protections and the legal rights that married couples have."[18] This rising level of Democratic support was frequently attributed to polls showing increased public acceptance of the idea of gay marriage

Obama Endorses Gay Marriage

In 2010 legislators in New Hampshire and Washington, D.C., passed bills legalizing same-sex marriage. Lawmakers in New York State followed suit in 2011, bringing the total number of states allowing gay marriage to six. The Obama administration also announced in 2011 that it would not defend DOMA in court proceedings, thus increasing the chance that the law might eventually be overturned. The U.S. military's controversial "Don't Ask, Don't Tell" policy toward gay service members also came to an end in September 2011. All of these developments pleased gay rights supporters.

The year 2012, though, was the one that has been widely characterized as a decisive turning point in the campaign for gay rights in general and gay marriage in particular. The year started

President Barack Obama hosted a reception for gay and lesbian activists at the White House in June 2012, just weeks after publicly stating that he thought gay couples should be able to get married.

on a down note for gay marriage advocates when Republican governor Chris Christie of New Jersey vetoed a bill that would have permitted same-sex marriage in that state. Gay marriage activists experienced another setback in May 2012, when voters in North Carolina passed a constitutional amendment banning same-sex marriage.

From that point forward, though, a series of major political triumphs lifted gay and straight supporters of same-sex marriage to unprecedented heights of happiness and confidence. On May 9, 2012, Obama endorsed same-sex marriage in an interview—becoming the first sitting president ever to take that position. Many conservative opponents described Obama's announcement as a declaration of war on traditional marriage and a cynical bid to get more money from gay donors for his reelection campaign.

Supporters of gay marriage hailed the announcement, however. "I was utterly unprepared for how psychologically transformative the moment would be," wrote Sullivan. "To have the president of the United States affirm my humanity—and the humanity of all gay Americans—was, unexpectedly, a watershed. He shifted the mainstream in one interview . . . [and] moved an entire party behind a position that only a few years ago was regarded as simply preposterous."[19] Indeed, the political impact of Obama's public statement was further underscored in September 2012, when the Democratic Party became the first major political party in U.S. history to formally endorse gay marriage in its party platform.

Election Results Please Gay Marriage Advocates

As the November 2012 elections approached, political analysts speculated about whether Obama's gay marriage stance would hurt him, help him, or make no difference to voters. They also wondered whether the decision by the president and his party to formally endorse same-sex marriage would have any impact on congressional elections or state-level ballot referenda on the issue.

The November 2012 elections did not decisively answer some of these questions, since Americans vote for political candidates for many different reasons. But the overall election results delighted gay and straight supporters of same-sex marriage. Obama won reelection by a comfortable margin, and congressional Democrats had a good night as well. Democrats increased their majority in the Senate and made gains in the Republican-controlled House of Representatives. Wisconsin voters also became the first in American history to elect an openly gay U.S. Senate candidate—Tammy Baldwin—to represent them in Washington, D.C.

Finally, gay marriage supporters expressed great satisfaction with the results of four state-level ballot referenda on same-sex

Gay Marriage Around the World

As of early 2013, twelve countries around the world had legalized same-sex marriage. In 2001 the Netherlands became the first country to recognize gay marriage. The most recent nation to do so was Brazil, which legalized gay marriage in 2011. Other countries that have taken this step are Belgium (in 2003), Canada (2005), Iceland (2010), Norway (2008), Portugal (2010), South Africa (2006), Spain (2005), and Sweden (2009). Nearly twenty other countries, including France, Germany, and the United Kingdom, have legalized civil unions for same-sex couples but have not approved gay marriage.

Homosexuality is still regarded as a criminal offense in many parts of the world, however—especially in Africa and the Middle East. In five countries— Iran, Saudi Arabia, Yemen, Mauritania, and Sudan—homosexuality is a crime punishable by death.

A lesbian couple exchange marriage vows in Sweden, one of eight countries that have legalized gay marriage.

unions. Voters in Maine, Maryland, and Washington State all approved same-sex marriage in their states. These three states thus became the first states in American history to approve same-sex marriage by popular vote (rather than through legislative acts or court orders). Minnesota voters also defeated a proposal to amend their state's constitution to prohibit same-sex marriage.

CHAPTER 3

The Case for Gay Marriage

Supporters of same-sex marriage in the United States are en-couraged by the shifting political and cultural tides of the past several years. They believe that growing public acceptance of the idea of gay marriage is due in great measure to the increased visibility of homosexual men and women in American politics, business, and community activities. Positive and sympathetic portrayals of gay people and homosexual relationships in American movies, television shows, and literature have also helped. Finally, gay marriage advocates insist that they have been able to change public perceptions because their arguments—detailed below—have simply been stronger than those presented by opponents of same-sex marriage.

A Question of Fairness and Compassion

Supporters of same-sex marriage often campaign for their cause by emphasizing themes of fairness and compassion. They say that gay couples who want to marry are pursuing the same thing that heterosexual couples have been enjoying for centuries—a union based on the desire for love, happiness, security, and fulfillment. "The fight for gay marriage is often portrayed in political terms—Democrat versus Republican, liberal versus conservative," wrote actress Cynthia Nixon, who married her lesbian partner in May 2012. "But for couples like us, this is about something simpler and more personal. I want to be married to my girlfriend. And I want us to have a ceremony. I want all our friends and family to come, and I want our kids to be there. . . . I want it to be a moment I will always remember. Till death do us part."[20]

The gay marriage campaign is not being waged solely by homosexual men and women, either. Many straight people have spoken out about their desire to see gay friends and neighbors have the option of entering into marriage relationships. "It was not until I was in college that I was aware of having gay friends," wrote journalist James Fallows, "and over the years, as my wife and I have celebrated their marriages (where that was legal) and their non-married partnerships (where it was not), I've come to understand that it is pointless, cruel, unfair, and wrong to deny them the satisfactions, and responsibilities, of committed married life."[21]

A demonstration for same-sex marriage rights takes place in California. Many straight people have spoken out about their desire to see gay friends, relatives, and neighbors have the option of entering into legal marital relationships.

A Civil Rights Issue

Advocates of gay marriage also frame the issue as one of basic equality. They argue that denying committed gay and lesbian couples the financial, emotional, and legal benefits of marriage makes them second-class citizens. It walls them off from utilizing rights that heterosexual married couples take for granted, including inheritance rights, the ability to seek child support, visitation rights, Social Security survivor benefits, health insurance coverage, and the right to make major medical decisions for their partners.

Seventy-one-year-old Marion Kenneally said that these legal rights were very important to her and her partner of twenty-six years, Anna Bissonette, when they were finally able to marry in 2004 in Massachusetts (the first state to legalize same-sex marriage). "We already felt married to each other physically, roman-

In 2004, when the state of Massachusetts legalized gay marriage, Anna Bissonette (pictured) was able to marry Marion Kenneally, her partner of twenty-six years.

tically, and spiritually," she explained. "What we gained under the law were some of the same rights and protections enjoyed by our straight relatives and friends who are married. . . . Our marriage gives us validation as a couple."[22]

GAY MARRIAGE AND SUFFRAGE

"The truth is that ending the exclusion of gay people from marriage does not change the 'definition' of marriage any more than allowing women to vote changed the 'definition' of voting."— Gay marriage advocate Evan Wolfson

Evan Wolfson. "Defending the Motion." *Economist*, January 5, 2011. www.economist .com/debate/days/view/634.

The inferior legal status of gay Americans in most states has led some allies of gay marriage to compare their cause to that of the African American civil rights movement of the 1950s and 1960s. During this era, black Americans and their white supporters protested against discriminatory municipal, state, and federal laws that had been in place since the earliest days of the United States' existence. These discriminatory laws extended to the area of sexual relations and marriage. Colonial, territorial, and state legislatures all passed laws outlawing interracial marriage, and by the time of the civil rights movement, interracial marriage was illegal in most American communities.

The civil rights movement broke down these marriage barriers, and in 1967 the U.S. Supreme Court declared all municipal and state laws banning interracial marriage (known as antimiscegenation laws) to be unconstitutional. Since that time, rates of interracial marriage in the United States have steadily grown. In 2010 the Pew Research Center reported that one out of twelve married couples in the United States were interracial couples.

Heterosexual mixed-race marriages are no longer even a source of controversy in most towns, cities, and households. One hundred years ago, interracial marriage was perceived by whites who controlled American politics and culture as an unthinkable and disgusting violation of the laws of nature and a threat to their society. Today, interracial marriages are just an unremarkable part of modern American life. According to a 2011 Gallup public opinion poll, in fact, 86 percent of Americans approve of interracial marriage.

According to African American journalist Ta-Nehisi Coates, bans on gay marriage are in some respects even worse than America's historical bans on interracial marriage. "The comparison with interracial marriage actually understates the evil of reserving marriage rights for certain classes of people," Coates writes. "Banning interracial marriage meant that most black people could not marry outside of their race. This was morally indefensible, but very different than a total exclusion of gays from the institution of marriage. Throughout much of America, gays are effectively banned from marrying, not simply certain types of people, *but any another compatible partner period.*"[23]

Finally, people who view same-sex marriage as a civil rights issue claim that such unions do not violate the rights of Americans who are opposed to the practice for religious or moral reasons. "Separation of church and state is a principle that allows Americans to support liberties and opportunities for all, even if they choose to live according to different values than those of their neighbors,"[24] writes journalist Samuel G. Freedman.

Addressing the Procreation Argument

Supporters of same-sex marriage have little regard or patience for the argument that marriage should be reserved for male-female relationships because those are the only ones that can naturally create children. Gay-marriage advocates acknowledge that many of the world's great religions emphasize the importance of creating children, a process sometimes known as procreation, in marriage arrangements.

But this argument has little weight for people who are not religious. Same-sex marriage, writes lesbian journalist E. J. Graff, is based instead on the idea that "marriage (and therefore sex) is justified not by reproduction but by love."[25]

In addition, people who are pro–gay marriage frequently assert that modern followers of religion pick and choose which

An NFL Player Weighs In on Gay Marriage

As the national debate over same-sex marriage has intensified, Americans from all walks of life have offered their opinions on the issue—including Chris Kluwe, then punter for the National Football League's Minnesota Vikings. Kluwe entered the national spotlight after he wrote a blistering, profanity-laced response to a Maryland state legislator who had asked the owner of the NFL's Baltimore Ravens to prevent the team's players from voicing support for civil unions in the state.

Kluwe published his open letter on Deadspin.com, a sports-oriented web site. Within a matter of days, it attracted national attention not only for its creative insults, but also for its ringing endorsement of gay marriage. "Why do you hate the fact that other people want a chance to live their lives and be happy, even though they may believe in something different than you, or act different than you?" Kluwe wrote. "You know what having [full legal rights that come with marriage] will make gays? Full-fledged American citizens just like everyone else, with the freedom to pursue happiness and all that entails. Do the civil-rights struggles of the past 200 years mean absolutely nothing to you?"

Kluwe's public stance was gratefully acknowledged by gay civil rights activists in Minnesota and across the nation. It has even been credited as a factor in the narrow defeat in November 2012 of a proposal to amend Minnesota's state constitution to outlaw gay marriage.

Quoted in Tony Gervino. "The Punter Makes His Point." *New York Times,* October 19, 2012. www.nytimes .com/2012/10/20/sports/football/punter-chris-kluwes -voice-is-heard-in-same-sex-marriage-debate.html ?pagewanted=all.

NFL punter Chris Kluwe speaks at the fifth annual PFLAG National Straight for Equality Awards ceremony in April 2013.

guidelines to heed. Modern Christians, for example, do not treat biblical injunctions against divorce or eating shellfish or pork as ironclad rules. Some supporters of gay marriage believe that it is hypocritical for modern Christians who eat shellfish or have gotten divorced to use Bible scriptures to condemn homosexuality or claim that marriages hinge on procreation.

Advocates of gay marriage also point out that heterosexual married couples who choose not to have children or are unable to have children because of advanced age or medical conditions (like sterility) are not barred from marriage. To the contrary, their weddings are celebrated just like any other. Supporters of same-sex marriage believe that gay and lesbian couples are entitled to the same treatment. "Sterile couples are allowed to marry in [the Catholic Church] and to have sex," wrote gay political writer Andrew Sullivan.

> So are couples in which the wife is post-menopausal. It's understood that such people have no choice in the matter. . . . They are just tragically unable, as the Church sees it, to experience the joy of a procreative married life. The question, of course, is Why doesn't this apply to homosexuals? . . . Why aren't they allowed to express their love as humanely as they possibly can, along with the infertile and the elderly?[26]

Many Americans who support gay marriage are also religiously devout themselves. These practicing Christians, Jews, and Muslims maintain that their efforts to legalize same-sex marriage are perfectly compatible with the values of love, compassion, and fidelity that all of these religious faiths emphasize. "Many gays and lesbians simply desire what their parents had, or could have had: fidelity, commitment, companionship, and mutual gratitude for their daily bread," wrote Catholic publisher and author Michael Leach. "They know that life is tough enough to get through alone. Like anyone who finds loving compatibility with another, gays want to partake in the good of God with a soul mate."[27]

Finally, gay marriage advocates point out that as a matter of law, civil marriage in America has not been justified solely by reproduction since 1965. That was the year that the U.S. Supreme Court struck down state laws that outlawed the sale of birth control materials to married couples.

Raising Healthy and Happy Children

Many gay men and women in the United States are raising children. About 2 million children in America, in fact, are being raised in LGBT (lesbian, gay, bisexual, and transgender) households, according to a 2011 study released by the Movement Advancement Project, the Family Equality Council, and the Center for American Progress. Some of these children come from previous heterosexual marriages or other relationships, while others come from artificial insemination procedures or adoption (although many states restrict adoption rights for LGBT couples).

A FORM OF GAY-BASHING

"A constitutional amendment banning same-sex marriage is a form of gay-bashing and it would do nothing at all to protect traditional marriages."—Coretta Scott King, civil rights activist and widow of Martin Luther King Jr.

Quoted in Patricia A. Gozemba and Karen Kahn. *Courting Equality: A Documentary History of America's First Legal Same-Sex Marriages.* Boston: Beacon Press, 2007, p. 65.

Gay marriage supporters strongly object to charges that same-sex parenting has negative psychological effects on children. To the contrary, they assert that studies have shown that children of gay and lesbian parents fare just as well in terms of academic and social achievement as other children. Studies have also found that children of gay parents are no more likely to identify themselves as gay than children of straight parents. Advocates of same-sex marriage also emphasize that organizations like the American Academy of Pediatrics, the Child Welfare League of America, and the American Psychological Association agree that same-sex couples are as capable of providing sound parenting as heterosexual couples.

Eagle scout and University of Iowa student Zach Wahls stands with his parents, Jacqueline Regars and Terry Wahls. Zach's January 2011 pro–gay marriage statement at a public hearing on a proposed constitutional amendment to ban gay marriage in Iowa became an overnight YouTube sensation.

This is certainly the position of Zach Wahls, who was raised by a lesbian couple who used artificial insemination to have both him and his younger sister. Wahls was an engineering student at the University of Iowa in January 2011 when he attended a public hearing on a proposed constitutional amendment to ban gay marriage in Iowa. Wahls' brief speech at the hearing became a YouTube sensation, in large part because it squarely addressed the issue of gay parenting:

> The question always comes down to, "Can gays even raise kids?" And the conversation gets quiet for a moment, because most people don't really have an answer. And then I raise my hand and say, "Well actually, I was raised by a gay couple, and I'm doing pretty well." I score in the 99th percentile on the ACT. I'm an Eagle Scout. I own and operate my own small business. If I was your son, Mr. Chairman, I believe I'd make you very proud. I'm not so different from any of your children. My family really isn't so different from yours. After all, your family doesn't derive its sense of worth from being told by the state, "You're married, congratulations!" The sense of family comes from the commitment we make to each other to work through the hard times so we can enjoy the good ones. It comes from the love that binds us. That's what makes a family. . . . Not once have I ever been confronted by an individual who realized independently that I was raised by a gay couple. And you know why? Because the sexual orientation of my parents has had zero impact on the content of my character. Thank you.[28]

Proponents of gay marriage also ask opponents to acknowledge that there are many adoptable children who wish every day to find adoptive or foster parents. Would opponents really rather keep those children in orphanages or foster care than in the warm and caring home of a same-sex couple? "Sexual orientation is fundamentally irrelevant to a person's capacity to be a good parent," states the National Center for Lesbian Rights (NCLR). "Social science research has confirmed what experience and common sense already suggest, namely, that love, stability, patience, and time to spend with a child are far more critical factors in being a good parent than a person's gender or sexual orientation."[29]

Gay rights advocate Evan Wolfson echoes this point. "There is no evidence to support the offensive proposition that only one size of family must fit all," he writes. "What counts is not family structure, but the quality of dedication, commitment, self-sacrifice, and love in the household." Wolfson also expresses bewilderment with conservative gay marriage opponents who extol the benefits of marriage to *heterosexual* couples. "Their position that marriage is good for everyone except lesbians and gay men . . . is puzzling," he says. "How does it help the children being raised by gay parents to deprive these children of the protections and support that would come to their families with marriage?[30]

Gay rights advocate Evan Wolfson spoke for many gay rights advocates when he said, "There is no evidence to support the offensive proposition that only one size of family must fit all. . . . What counts is not family structure, but the quality of dedication, commitment, self-sacrifice, and love in the household."

No Threat to Traditional Marriage

Supporters of same-sex marriage—or marriage equality, as they sometimes call it—also reject accusations that gay marriage poses a threat to traditional heterosexual marriage. They freely acknowledge that traditional marriage faces many threats in the twenty-first century, including rising rates of infidelity and substance abuse, economic uncertainties, and popular reality TV shows, movies, and other entertainment that trivialize the institution. They agree that divorce rates are too high. But they say that these problems were around long before the gay marriage debate heated up.

A CONSERVATIVE ENDORSEMENT OF GAY MARRIAGE

"A gay or lesbian couple may love each other as deeply as any two people. . . . The conservative course is not to banish gay people from making such commitments. It is to expect that they make such commitments. We shouldn't just allow gay marriage. We should insist on gay marriage. We should regard it as scandalous that two people could claim to love each other and not want to sanctify their love with marriage and fidelity."—Conservative columnist David Brooks

David Brooks. "The Power of Marriage." *New York Times*, November 22, 2003. www .nytimes.com/2003/11/22/opinion/the-power-of-marriage.html.

People who support gay marriage also mock self-proclaimed defenders of traditional marriage such as conservative radio host Rush Limbaugh and Republican politician Newt Gingrich, both of whom have been divorced multiple times. "The Traditional Marriage movement is led by people who discard their wives and get new, younger replacements the way most people change underwear," charges liberal journalist Glenn Greenwald. "That's how so many Americans sit on their sofas next to their second and third spouses, with their step-children and half-siblings surrounding them, and explain—without any recognition of the irony—that they're against same-sex marriage because they believe the law should only recognize Traditional Marriages."[31]

Refuting the "Slippery Slope" Charge

Opponents of same-sex marriage have occasionally argued that if gay marriage is legalized across the United States, then marriages between close family relatives (incest) or three or more people (polygamy) might come next. This is sometimes referred to as the "slippery slope" argument against gay marriage. Supporters of gay marriage are openly contemptuous of these kinds of charges. "The hidden assumption of the argument which brackets gay marriage with polygamous or incestuous marriage is that homosexuals want the right to marry anybody they fall for," writes gay author Jonathan Rauch. "But, of course, heterosexuals are currently denied that right. They cannot marry their immediate family or all their sex partners. What homosexuals are asking for is the right to marry, not anybody they love, but *somebody* they love, which is not at all the same thing. . . . This is like arguing, "Once gay marriage is legal, how can you stop people from marrying their dog?" To such an argument, the appropriate response is, Don't be ridiculous."

Jonathan Rauch. "Marrying Somebody." *Same-Sex Marriage: Pro and Con; A Reader.* Rev. ed. Edited by Andrew Sullivan. New York: Vintage, 2004.

People who support gay marriage do not expect same-sex marriages to be magically immune from the hardships, temptations, and communication breakdowns that damage many traditional marriages. Advocates do not see, though, how the existence of gay married couples will have any impact on the success or failure of straight marriages. "Heterosexual marriage will still flourish with its statistical failures," writes liberal Protestant minister Howard Moody. "The only difference will be that some homosexual couples will join them and probably account for about the same number of failed relationships."[32]

Gay Marriage as a Stabilizing Force in Society

Advocates for same-sex marriage have also fought back hard against arguments that allowing gay men and lesbians to marry their same-gender partners will erode the moral foundations of American society.

As Sullivan notes, opponents have long claimed that the gay lifestyle is "one in which emotional commitments are fleeting, promiscuous sex is common, disease is rampant, social ostracism is common, and standards of public decency, propriety, and self-restraint are flouted."[33] Yet supporters point out that many gay couples have remained devoted to each other for years or even decades—despite the absence of laws or ceremonies that make their bond official, and despite outright hostility from many sectors of American society.

Sullivan also charges that conservatives have a lot of nerve criticizing temporary homosexual relationships at the same time that they try to keep gays from participating in marriage—an institution that places an incredibly high value on being faithful to one's sexual and romantic partner. "Here was a minority asking for responsibility and commitment and integration," Sullivan writes, "and conservatives were determined to keep them in

This Los Angeles demonstration against gay marriage took place in 2004. Proponents of gay marriage contend that allowing same-sex marriages will have no negative effect on heterosexual marriage.

isolation. . . . What they could not see was that the conservative tradition of reform and inclusion, of social change through existing institutions, of the family and personal responsibility, all led inexorably toward civil marriage for gays."[34]

Graff believes that much of the conservative opposition to same-sex marriage stems from a recognition that it will make gays seem less strange and foreign to straight Americans. It will thus result in greater acceptance of gay and lesbian people in general. "The right wing would much rather see outré [bizarre or unusual] urban queers throwing drunken kisses off bar floats than have two nice married girls move in next door, with or without papoose [child], demonstrating to every neighborhood kid that a good marriage is defined from the inside out."[35]

Supporters of gay marriage insist that the practice has no negative impact on the relationships that straight people have with their spouses, children, or communities. They further argue that same-sex marriage makes *positive* contributions to the health, vitality, and stability of neighborhoods, towns, and cities. "We know enough about evil in an evil world to know that its enemy and antidote is love," says writer Lance Morrow. "Whatever fosters love (generosity, charity, forbearance, decency, human connection, understanding) is good. If marriage adds to the overall sum of love—and therefore, of good—in the world, then legalizing gay marriages adds to the sum and improves the world. If marriage does not add to the overall sum of love and constructive good, then the institution of marriage is not worth protecting."[36]

THE CASE AGAINST GAY MARRIAGE

Although the idea of same-sex marriage has gained greater acceptance in the United States in recent years, it is still an enormously controversial issue. Millions of Americans remain strongly opposed to the idea, and they vow to continue the fight to keep marriage an institution that can only be entered into by male-female couples. "Giving 'legal sanction' to homosexuals marrying and calling their contract a 'marriage' does not make it a marriage," writes Orson Scott Card, a well-known science fiction writer and activist opposed to same-sex marriage. "It simply removes *marriage* as a legitimate word for the real thing."[37]

Gay Marriage as an Immoral and Sinful Institution

Most of the resistance to gay marriage is founded on deeply held beliefs that homosexuality itself is immoral. Among conservative Christians, who play an extremely influential role in the battle against gay marriage, homosexuality is even worse than immoral. In their view, people who engage in homosexual sexual activities are sinners who are flouting essential Biblical teachings about how human beings should conduct their lives, raise their families, and govern their sexuality. This faith-based aversion to homosexuality is sometimes summed up by the slogan that God made Adam and Eve—not Adam and Steve.

Foes of gay marriage also emphasize that most of America's laws and codes of behavior are clearly patterned after biblical concepts of morality. "Try looking at the criminal code of any state or the federal system and tell me it isn't based on morality," writes conservative political commentator David Limbaugh.

Conservative pundit William Bennett has stated that for same-sex marriage to become fully integrated into American culture, society would have to accept that centuries of tradition regarding marriage as being between a man and a woman has been wrong.

"Look further into our civil law and try to deny that much, if not most, of tort law and contract law, not to mention property law, are rooted in our traditional (Biblical) moral beliefs."[38]

Limbaugh and others argue that if gay marriage becomes the law of the land, it could spark a tragic erosion of other laws and codes that have served the country so well. "If we remove that foundation [of biblical morality]," writes Limbaugh, "the fabric of our society will unravel, and we'll eventually lose our liberties—ironically, at the hands of those claiming to champion freedom."[39]

Conservative writer and cultural critic William J. Bennett has written that if same-sex marriage becomes fully integrated into American culture, society would have to accept several basic assumptions:

> It would have to accept that the Jewish and Christian understanding of marriage and family life is thoroughly misguided—simply wrong. It would have to accept that humankind itself has been misguided—wrong—to

recognize something different, special, or sacred about the sexual union of husband (male) and wife (female). It would have to accept that marriage has nothing to do with the different, complementary nature of men and women. It would have to accept that homosexuality is equal in all important ways to heterosexuality. . . . Proponents of same-sex marriage are hardly qualified to dictate to others what constitutes its central meaning. . . . What arguments would they invoke? Tradition? Religion? The time-honored definition of the family? These are the very pillars they have already destroyed.[40]

The Debate over Conversion Therapy

Conversion therapies are controversial psychological treatments designed to change sexual orientation. They have been hailed by conservative Christian groups and other critics of gay lifestyles and same-sex marriage as a way to "cure" homosexuals of their unnatural sexual urges and convert them to heterosexuality. Some of the leading spokespeople for conversion therapy, in fact, describe themselves as "ex-gays" who learned how to change their sexual orientation. Conservation therapy, which is also sometimes called reparative therapy, has been used to treat thousands—perhaps even tens of thousands—of children and adults who are sexually attracted to people of their own gender.

Leading medical and mental health organizations across the country, however, have roundly condemned the practice as harmful. Groups such as the American Psychological Association, the American Medical Association, the American Academy of Pediatrics, the American Association for Marriage and Family Therapy, and the American School Counselor Association have all firmly rejected conversion therapy, as have some progressive religious groups. These organizations have joined with gay Americans who say that homosexuality is not a disorder or disease that needs to be cured. Critics charge that conversion therapy is actually incredibly destructive to the psychological health of youth and adults who undergo treatment. In many cases, they say, people undergoing such treatment are at higher risk of depression and suicide.

Marriage Is for Procreation

Arguments made by religious conservatives against same-sex marriage also focus on the fact that man-woman relationships can naturally produce children, while same-gender couples cannot procreate without assistance from modern science. This is an important distinction for many people who believe that the ultimate purpose of marriage is to create and nurture children. Political commentator Maggie Gallagher is one of America's most prominent defenders of traditional marriage. "For millions of Americans," she writes,

> the sense that marriage is sacred, that it involves something foundational to our culture, is rooted in human nature: Unions of husband and wife really are different from other loving relationships; they are necessary to the whole future of society in a way other relationships, however loving, are not. Gay marriage is rooted in a false equation: Loving a man is not the same as loving a woman; a sexual union that can give rise to children is fundamentally different in kind than a union not so freighted, for good and for ill, with the fact of procreativity.[41]

GAY MARRIAGE AS A SELFISH INSTITUTION

"It's all about them. The stated justifications for same-sex marriage have nothing to do with how this approach to mating can contribute to the common good, but everything to do with what society can, or must, do for the couple."—Conservative scholar and writer Robert W. Patterson

Robert W. Patterson. "Why Gay Marriage Doesn't Measure Up." *Human Events*, March 22, 2004. www.humanevents.com/2004/03/22/why-gay-marriage-doesnt-measure-up/.

Advocates of gay marriage have pointed out that some heterosexual couples are unable to have children because of infertility due to age or medical condition, yet they are not attacked or criticized by opponents of same-sex marriage. If procreation is so important, ask gay marriage advocates, then why are these

America's Best-Known Opponent of Gay Marriage

Maggie Gallagher is one of America's best-known social critics and political activists. She fiercely opposes same-sex marriage at the same time that she champions the virtues of traditional marriage and sexual abstinence outside of marriage. In 2007 she founded the influential National Organization for Marriage, and she served as president of that influential organization until 2010.

"In her books and newspaper columns, and above all in her fundraising and political organizing, Gallagher has done more than any American to stop same-sex marriage,"[1] writes journalist Mark Oppenheimer.

The foundation for Gallagher's firm stance on gay marriage is her deeply held belief that married male-female couples provide the healthiest—and the only natural—environment for childrearing and child development. "Not all marriage systems look like our own," she says. "Yet everywhere, in isolated mountain valleys, parched deserts, jungle thickets and broad plains, people have come up with some [heterosexual] version of this thing called marriage. Why? Because sex between men and women makes babies, that's why."[2]

1. Mark Oppenheimer. "The Making of Gay Marriage's Top Foe." *Salon,* February 8, 2012. www.salon.com /2012/02/08/the_making_of_gay_marriages_top _foe/.
2. Maggie Gallagher. "What Marriage Is For." *Weekly Standard,* August 4, 2003. Reprinted in *Same-Sex Marriage: Pro and Con; A Reader.* Rev. ed. Edited by Andrew Sullivan. New York: Vintage, 2004, p. 267.

Maggie Gallagher founded the antigay National Organization for Marriage in 2007.

childless unions celebrated and respected? Defenders of traditional marriage respond that the situations are totally different. A 2010 essay written by conservative scholars, for example, compares heterosexual marriages to a baseball team:

> A baseball team has its characteristic structure largely because of its orientation to winning games; it involves developing and sharing one's athletic skills in the way best suited for honorably winning . . . . But such development and sharing are possible and inherently valuable for teammates even when they lose their games. Just so, marriage has its characteristic structure largely because of its orientation to procreation; it involves developing and sharing one's body and whole self in the way best suited for honorable parenthood—among other things, permanently and exclusively. But such development and sharing, including the bodily union of the generative act, are possible and inherently valuable for spouses even when they do not conceive children.[42]

Gallagher also notes that "every marriage between a man and a woman is capable of giving any child they create or adopt a mother and a father. Every marriage between a man and a woman discourages either from creating fatherless children outside the marriage vow. In this sense, neither older married couples nor childless husbands and wives publicly challenge or dilute the core meaning of marriage."[43]

The Catholic Church has taken a leading role in this argument. Its position is consistent with its general "pro-life" orientation, which includes strong opposition to abortion and birth control measures. "Children are meant to be the gift of the permanent and exclusive union of a husband and a wife," stated the U.S. Conference of Catholic Bishops (USCCB) in 2009. "The true nature of marriage, lived in openness to life, is a witness to the precious gift of the child and to the unique roles of a mother and father. Same-sex unions are incapable of such a witness." The USCCB added that equating homosexual partnerships with traditional marriages diminishes the importance of producing children, which it called "fundamental to the existence and well-being of society as a whole."[44]

The U.S. Conference of Catholic Bishops declared in 2009 that "children are meant to be the gift of the permanent and exclusive union of a husband and a wife." It added that equating homosexual partnerships with traditional marriages diminishes the importance of producing children, which it called "fundamental to the existence and well-being of society as a whole."

A Threat to America's Children

Opponents of gay marriage frequently charge that children in households that are missing either a mother or a father do not do as well socially or academically as peers who live with both male and female parents. They grant that many children raised in single-parent homes and homes maintained by same-sex couples grow up to become happy, productive, and heterosexual adults. But they say that research has shown that children who grow up in households with gay parents have a greater likelihood of developing psychological problems and emotional issues related to sexual development. Some organizations and websites devoted to the preservation of traditional marriage even relate stories of lesbian and gay parents who are so hostile to the opposite gender that they create severe emotional problems for their children.

These studies have been criticized as flawed by gay marriage advocates, who cite other research indicating that children in same-sex households fare just as well as those from traditional families. Opponents of same-sex marriage stand by their position, however, and assert that problems associated with gay parents raising children will become more evident over time. "It is the powerful dynamic of a mother, father, and children that creates those bonds of family that form the bedrock of all societies and provide the best environment for raising children—as social science has clearly demonstrated," writes Tony Perkins, president of a conservative Christian organization called the Family Research Council (FRC). "Children need both a mom and a dad, not just two adults. There are compelling, scientific reasons to define marriage as the union of a man and a woman.

Family Research Council president Tony Perkins asserts that there are compelling scientific reasons to define marriage as the union of a man and a woman.

They expose the arguments of same-sex advocates as self-serving talking points with no basis in human nature and American history."[45]

HATING THE SIN, NOT THE SINNER

"I am not anti-gay. . . . Those of us who fear the consequences of redefining marriage—asking children if they hope to marry a boy or a girl when they get older, banning religious adoption agencies from placing children first with a married man and woman, denying the importance of both sexes in making families, choosing boys to be high-school prom queens and girls to be high-school prom kings, and much more—must make it clear that we regard homosexuals as fellow human beings created in God's image just as heterosexuals are."—Conservative commentator Dennis Prager

Dennis Prager. "Conservatives and Gays: Where Do We Stand?" *National Review Online,* May 9, 2012. www.nationalreview.com/articles/299401/conservatives-and -gays-where-do-we-stand-dennis-prager#.

Critics of same-sex marriage often say that men and women who enter into homosexual relationships are placing a higher value on their own sexual desires than on making sure that their children—whether from a previous heterosexual relationship or from adoption—are raised in the best family setting. "The marriage idea," said Gallagher, "is that children need mothers and fathers, that societies need babies, and that adults have an obligation to shape their sexual behavior so as to give their children stable families in which to grow up."[46]

A Threat to Wider Society and Traditional Families

Opponents of same-sex marriage also warn that acceptance of the practice will negatively affect American society and traditional families in a variety of important ways. "While marriage has a private aspect, it is a public institution that impacts the entire society," writes conservative lawyer and scholar Mathew D. Staver. "We cannot isolate marriage inside the four walls of a home. Our attitude and public policies toward marriage will affect the culture."[47]

One accusation leveled by foes of gay marriage is that many homosexuals—and gay men in particular—dislike the idea of sexually monogamous relationships. One fear is that this alleged dissatisfaction with keeping only one sexual partner will spread to heterosexual marriages, triggering even higher levels of adultery than already exist. Such behavior, critics charge, will also stunt the emotional development and warp the sexual outlooks and behavior of younger generations. In the view of gay marriage critics, such an alteration of family "norms"—expected standards of behavior in a society—would be catastrophic. "To be sure, some advocates of same-sex marriage hope that heterosexual marital norms of monogamy and fidelity would be transferred to same-sex unions," admits Mollie Ziegler Hemingway in *Christianity Today.*

> But since these norms are based on the ideal that marriage is the union of a man and woman making a permanent and exclusive commitment for the purpose of bearing and rearing children, it would be irrational to expect same-sex partners—whose sexual relations bear no risk of procreation—to share the same norms. . . . Same-sex partnerships would teach people that marriage is fundamentally about the emotional union of adults and not primarily about the bodily union of man and wife (let alone the children who result from such a union). The norms of permanence, monogamy, and fidelity would make less sense under such a change.[48]

Opponents of same-sex marriage also ridicule claims made by gay rights advocates that permitting gay unions would have no effect on straight couples and their families. They worry that if gay marriage gains legal and popular acceptance, people who legitimately criticize it as unnatural or sinful will increasingly be unfairly slandered as narrow-minded or bigoted. "Gay marriage," argues Gallagher, "will almost certainly lead to new efforts to stigmatize and repress the traditional view of marriage, both in law and in culture." In fact, she claims, this phenomenon is already evident. Gallagher believes that gay marriage advocates have adopted the stance that "if you try to stand for the idea that marriage matters because children need a mom and dad, and get dubbed a bigot, it's your own fault for not getting on the gay marriage bandwagon."[49]

Many conservatives fear that social acceptance of gay marriage will further deteriorate the institution of marriage.

Another criticism is that treasured religious liberties and parental rights will come under assault if gay marriage becomes widely accepted. "When marriage is redefined (whether by a vote of the legislature or by a court mandating the change), same-sex marriage becomes the law of the state and something all in-state levels of government must accommodate and promote as equal to marriage between a man and a woman," according to Focus on the Family, a conservative organization devoted to various social issues. "While that might not sound so bad on the surface, that means your child's public school could become a place where same-sex marriage is taught—regardless of your values or beliefs, or whether you want your child to be learning about the topic at all."[50] Conservative critics of same-sex marriage also warn that legal recognition of such unions could even force schools, charities, adoption agencies, and summer camps—including those owned and operated by religious organizations that are deeply opposed to gay marriage—to offer marital benefits to gay couples or risk fines, loss of public funding, or loss of operating licenses.

An Ever-Expanding Definition of Marriage?

Opponents of gay marriage have repeatedly said that legally sanctioning same-sex marriages could open the floodgates to acceptance of other types of relationships that American society (and most other world cultures) has long viewed as immoral or even evil. If the definition of marriage is going to be reshaped to include gay and lesbian couples, they ask, then what is to stop a campaign for acceptance of incestuous partners or groups of three or more partners?

Proponents of gay marriage contend that such comparisons are absurd, but defenders of traditional marriage are not so sure. "To those who object to comparing gay marriage to widely-rejected sexual preferences, it should be pointed out that until very recent times the very suggestion that two men or two women could 'marry' was itself greeted with scorn," states the Family Research Council. "This nebulous, free-for-all model of the family looms ahead for our society unless a bulwark is created in the form of a constitutional amendment protecting marriage. . . . Where do we draw the limits on who can marry?"[51]

Bennett has voiced similar concerns about the precedent that could be set if marriage in the United States is redefined to include same-sex couples:

There are no principled grounds on which advocates of same-sex marriage can oppose the marriage of two consenting brothers. . . . Or to a man who wants a consensual polygamous [multi-wife] arrangement. Or to a father and his adult daughter. Any of these people may desire to enter into a lifetime of loving, faithful commitment; may believe that without marriage their ability to love and be loved is incomplete, that society is preventing their happiness, and that they deserve to be treated equally by the government to which they pay their taxes and bear allegiance. These are the same arguments used by proponents of same-sex marriage to justify their cause.[52]

Opponents of gay marriage say that legalizing same-sex unions could lead to people's marrying their relatives or even their pets.

Gay Marriage Is Not a Civil Rights Issue

Finally, large numbers of Americans who oppose same-sex marriage reject the idea that denying lesbians or gays the ability to marry one another deprives them of civil rights guaranteed in the U.S. Constitution. Homosexual men and women already have the right to marry—they just have to marry people of the opposite sex. According to defenders of traditional marriage such as Gallagher, these arrangements sometimes can be very successful. "Our laws do not require a person to marry the individual to whom he or she is most erotically attracted, so long as he or she is willing to promise sexual fidelity, mutual caretaking, and shared parenting of any children of the marriage,"[53] she states.

Opponents also believe that gay advocates sometimes exaggerate the legal and financial disadvantages that unmarried same-sex couples face. They point out, for example, that individuals can make joint property ownership arrangements regardless of their marital status. They can also file legal documents authorizing their partner to make health care decisions on their behalf in many parts of the country, and they are generally free to leave money and possessions to anyone they want in their wills.

Some observers also assert that gay advocates who call for "equal rights" regarding marriage misunderstand the issue. "If someone wants to argue that two people who have not in the past been recognized as marriage partners should now be recognized as marriage partners, one must demonstrate that marriage law (not civil rights law) has overlooked or misidentified something that it should not have overlooked or misidentified," writes James W. Skillen. "The much disputed question of whether same-sex relationships are morally good or bad, healthy or unhealthy, is beside the point." According to Skillen and other critics, the appeal now being made for homosexual marriage rights asks judges and lawmakers to ignore the obvious differences between heterosexual and homosexual relationships so that gay men and lesbian women can call their relationships whatever they want to call them. "If homosexual relationships are, in this manner, legally recognized as marriages," Skillen concludes, "the only thing that will change is that the law will mistakenly use the word 'marriage' to refer to two different kinds of sexually intimate human relationships."[54]

Critics of the same-sex marriage movement are convinced that civil liberties are not the issue that Americans should be worried about when they consider legally recognizing gay and lesbian unions as equal to male-female marriages. Instead, they believe that Americans need to focus on how gay marriage would destabilize society and the traditional family unit for future generations. "Anyone who recognizes the critical significance of strong marriages and families to the well being of children and the social health of the nation should shudder at the prospect of a radical redefinition of the already much-battered institution of marriage," insists conservative scholar Robert P. George. "We need policies that uphold and strengthen marriage, not those that further erode it in our law and culture."[55]

CHAPTER 5

THE FUTURE OF GAY MARRIAGE

Opinions differ greatly on the future of gay marriage in the United States. Even within the pro–gay marriage and anti–gay marriage camps, a wide variety of perspectives can be found. Many people who are supportive of same-sex marriage believe that the tide has decisively turned in their favor and that gay marriage will eventually be on the same legal footing as marriages between men and women across the entire United States. Other supporters are more skeptical, given the deep opposition to gay marriage that exists in many rural and conservative parts of the country.

Similarly, opponents of gay marriage look to the future with varying levels of anxiety. Some activists insist that a backlash against gay marriage is brewing, and they say that same-sex versions of traditional marriage will never be accepted in some parts of America. Critics like conservative political commentator George Will, however, believe that the fact that young Americans are far more supportive of gay marriage than older generations does not bode well for same-sex marriage opponents. "Quite literally," said Will in 2012, "the opposition to gay marriage is dying."[56]

Supporters Look Forward

The November 2012 election results in the United States gave great encouragement to Americans who support gay marriage. The reelection of President Barack Obama, who only five months earlier had become the first U.S. president to express support for same-sex marriage, delighted many gay and straight Obama supporters who worried that his stance on the issue might hurt him on election night. Advocates of gay marriage also celebrated the passage of three state initiatives in Maryland, Washington, and Maine to legalize same-sex marriage and the defeat in Minnesota of a proposed constitutional amendment to prohibit gay marriage. In surveying these results, gay writer and activist E.J. Graff pronounced herself "stunned to discover that Americans have moved farther and faster on marriage equality than I had dared to dream. . . . The world has changed. Ten American states have declared that I'm a full human being, a full citizen, with the right to love."[57]

Conservative columnist George Will believes that the fact that young Americans are far more supportive of gay marriage than older generations does not bode well for same-sex-marriage opponents.

A great many supporters of same-sex marriage now believe that "marriage equality has passed the tipping point," in Graff's words. They expect that gay marriage will garner additional victories in the courts and on state ballots in the years to come. Many of them also expect the passage of new legislation at the federal level that will pave the way for full legal recognition of same-sex marriages performed anywhere in the United States. The bottom line, say optimistic advocates, is that the majority of U.S. states will fully embrace marriage equality by the close of this decade. From there, they suggest, even deeply conservative "red" states will gradually fall in line and accept same-sex marriage.

Members of the Lesbian & Gay Band Association march in President Obama's second inaugural parade in 2013. Months before the election, Obama came out in support of gay marriage—the first American president to do so.

"One day, not long from now, it will be hard to remember what worried people so much about gay and lesbian couples committing themselves to marriage," wrote social critic Margaret Talbot in 2012. "Same-sex marriage is a historical inevitability—and what people say about it now, for and against, will be seen in that light." Talbot predicted that the U.S. Supreme Court will ultimately "do the right thing" and support same-sex marriage. "As in the *Loving* decision [which struck down laws against interracial marriage in 1967], the Court will reaffirm that the 'freedom to marry has long been recognized as one of the vital personal rights essential to the orderly pursuit of happiness by free men.' And it will finally uphold that freedom for gay and lesbian Americans."[58]

A CALL TO LEGALIZE GAY MARRIAGE

"[The U.S. Supreme Court] justices have a third option: upholding DOMA, Proposition 8 or both. Choosing that way would be a historic mistake. The court's job is to determine judges' proper role in moving the country away from discrimination, not to enshrine that discrimination in constitutional doctrine. However the court rules, its decision will be a guidepost on a road that eventually ends in legal and social acceptance of equal rights. It should not point backward."—*Washington Post* editorial board

Washington Post Editorial Board. "The Supreme Court's Options on Gay Marriage." *Washington Post,* December 12, 2012. http://articles.washingtonpost.com/2012-12-12 /opinions/35789142_1_doma-defense-of-marriage-act-marriage-equality.

Conservatives Urge Continued Resistance

Some opponents of same-sex marriage share the belief that the tide has decisively and permanently turned against them on this issue. But others who oppose elevating gay marriage to the same legal, moral, and cultural status as straight marriage have signaled that they have no intention of dropping their objections.

Many of these critics claim that gay rights supporters have been too quick to claim victory. They note that as of 2012, thirty states still have bans on gay marriage enshrined in their

Despite the changing national political landscape on gay marriage, antigay groups vow to continue to fight against gay marriage in individual states.

constitutions (twenty of these states also ban civil unions). Opponents of same-sex marriage also argue that other major social issues—most notably abortion—have been fiercely debated for decades, with neither side gaining a decisive advantage. Conservatives are particularly quick to note that ever since the U.S. Supreme Court legalized abortion across the country in 1973's *Roe v. Wade* decision, abortion opponents have managed to pass a wide range of state laws placing restrictions on access to the procedure. By 2012 four states had only one surgical-abortion clinic in operation within their borders, and the total number of abortion providers nationwide fell from more than 2,900 in 1982 to less than 1,800 in 2008 (the last year for which statistics are available).[59]

Opponents of same-sex marriage such as Tony Perkins, president of the Family Research Council, have insisted that gay marriage will experience a similar backlash once its full ramifications become visible. According to the *New York Times,* Perkins has predicted that "as people see what he called the consequences of same-sex marriage—grade schools' endorsing homosexuality, business owners and religious institutions forced to act against their religious beliefs—opposition will rebound. Rights advocates say such conflicts are rare and not caused by marriage laws."[60]

Other Americans who have stood against same-sex marriage have also urged their allies not to lose hope—and warned their adversaries against overconfidence. "Why do gay marriage advocates believe their victory is inevitable?" asks attorney and political commentator David French.

> Why do they think gay marriage will—over the long term—escape the ideological polarization that's gripped America on virtually every other issue of consequence? Isn't it far more likely that differing attitudes on marriage will merge into the rest of the ideological package that separates red [conservative states] from blue [liberal states]? . . . The Left is fooling itself if it thinks the argument for redefining marriage has the same moral or legal force as the battle for racial equality. . . . Barring Supreme Court action or a near-total cultural triumph of one side over the other, the America of 2032 will likely look a great deal like the America of 2012. Ladies and gentlemen, welcome to the stalemate.[61]

Awaiting the Supreme Court's Decision

In late 2012 the Supreme Court decided to review two major legal cases related to same-sex marriage. One of these cases is a legal challenge to California's Proposition 8, a constitutional ban on gay marriage that was passed in 2008. The other is a legal challenge to the Defense of Marriage Act (DOMA), a 1996 federal law that denies favorable tax treatment and federal health and pension benefits to legally married same-sex couples.

Speculation was rampant from both sides of the issue about how the Court might rule: The Court could legalize same-sex

A Historic Policy Change for Washington National Cathedral

In January 2013 the Washington National Cathedral in Washington, D.C., announced it would begin hosting gay marriage ceremonies. "We enthusiastically affirm each person as a beloved child of God—and doing so means including the full participation of gays and lesbians in the life of this spiritual home for the nation," declared the Reverend Gary Hall, dean of the cathedral.

Hall's announcement attracted national attention because of the church's prominent role as a symbolic house of prayer for both celebrations and tragedies in American history. Major events held at the cathedral have included funer-als and memorial services for numerous presidents (most recently the funeral of Gerald Ford in 2007), post-inauguration prayer services (most recently for Barack Obama in 2013), and national memorial services for astronaut Neil Armstrong and the victims of the September 11, 2001, terrorist attacks. The cathedral is part of the U.S. Episcopal Church, which is the largest Christian denomination in the United States that has ordained gay priests and bishops.

Washington National Cathedral. "Washington National Cathedral to Celebrate Same-Sex Weddings," January 9, 2013. www.nationalcathedral.org/press /PR-60QF1-310018.shtml.

A prayer service is held for same-sex families at the Washington National Cathedral. In January 2013 the church announced it would start conducting gay marriage ceremonies.

marriage nationwide, a ruling that would give gay and lesbian Americans a historic victory. This would most likely be accomplished by handing down a sweeping ruling that establishes gay marriage as constitutionally protected under the Fourteenth Amendment. But gay rights advocates and critics of gay marriage also recognize that the conservative-leaning Court could hand down a decision defining marriage as the exclusive province of male-female couples. Supporters of gay marriage acknowledge that such a decision would be devastating, especially given the movement's recent gains at the ballot box and in public opinion polls. "I think any time gay issues go to the U.S. Supreme Court we are all filled with anxiety because you never know," said John Duran, a West Hollywood, California, councilman and supporter of gay rights. "We have a lot of anxiety because we realize whatever decision they make, if it's adverse, we have to live with it for a generation."[62]

A HAZY LEGAL FUTURE FOR ALL "FAMILY STRUCTURES"

"Same-sex marriage is a new family form that seems destined to gain increasing legal and social acceptance. . . . These household forms remain very much a set of works in progress, 'incomplete institutions' in both law and culture. That very incompleteness, however, also heightens the possibility that the regulation of same-sex relationships will influence the law governing all family structures in ways that we cannot yet foresee."—Georgetown University law professor Nan D. Hunter

Nan D. Hunter. "The Future Impact of Same-Sex Marriage: More Questions than Answers." *Georgetown Law Journal,* vol. 100, no. 6, 2012, pp. 1878–1879. http://george townlawjournal.org/files/2012/08/1Hunter.pdf.

A third possibility mentioned by some legal analysts is that the Court might issue extremely narrow decisions on both cases that would not really settle the matter one way or the other. According to *Forbes,* constitutional law scholar William Eskridge and other legal experts believe that "the cases leave the high court plenty of escape hatches from taking a big step the country may not be ready for yet."[63]

As it turned out, the Court's ruling on June 26, 2013, was historic, although not as earth-shaking as it could have been. The decision was read by Justice Anthony Kennedy, often considered the Court's swing vote. In both cases the decision was five to four. The Court ruled that discrimination against same-sex couples' eligibility for marital benefits available to opposite-sex couples was unconstitutional. Thus same-sex couples will be able to receive or share in their spouse's benefits. The Court declined to rule on the California Prop 8 case on a technicality, which left the lower court victory intact, thus allowing gay marriage in California.

Possible Futures for Marriage in America

Americans on all sides of the gay marriage debate describe starkly different versions of the United States, depending on how the nation ultimately decides to handle the gay marriage issue. Opponents believe that a rejection of same-sex marriage will protect and strengthen traditional marriage and encourage a renewed emphasis on personal responsibility in American society. "Institutions [such as marriage] tend to be strongest when they make significant moral demands, and weaker when they pre-emptively accommodate themselves to human nature," wrote conservative columnist Ross Douthat. "A successful marital culture depends not only on a general ideal of love and commitment, but on specific promises, exclusions, and taboos. And the less specific and more inclusive an institution becomes, the more likely people are to approach it casually, if they enter it at all."[64]

Conservative critics like Maggie Gallagher continue to maintain that the institution of marriage will be doomed if marriages of lesbian women and gay men are elevated to the same legal and cultural position as marriages between heterosexual men and women. "Gay marriage is not just a tiny number of extra people in an existing institution, but a fundamental revision of marriage," she writes. "The distinctions between same-sex and opposite-sex unions are not irrational or arbitrary, they are real and rooted in human nature in ways that government fiat cannot overturn. . . . Take the woman out of the wedding, and marriage is no longer a universal human institution, necessary to the future of the whole society, indeed all of humanity. Cut off from its deep roots in human nature, marriage loses its past, and quite possibly, its future. We shall see."[65]

Advocates of same-sex marriage have an entirely different view. Supporters maintain that the spread of same-sex unions will strengthen marriage as an institution and bring America closer to its goal of providing full equality for all of its citizens. Gay historian George Chauncey admits that "no one can pre-

In 2013 the U.S. Supreme Court ruled that Section 3 of the Defense of Marriage Act was unconstitutional in banning same-sex partners from receiving marriage benefits.

Pope Benedict XVI Speaks Out Against Gay Marriage

On December 21, 2012, Pope Benedict XVI used the traditional Christmas message issued by the pope every year to deliver a stern repudiation of same-sex marriage. Pope Benedict has long been known for his opposition to homosexuality and gay marriage, but in 2012 he expressed these beliefs on multiple occasions. In his Christmas message, in fact, he delivered what some observers called his strongest remarks yet on gay marriage. The pope's speech bluntly described gay marriage as an attack on traditional families and a genuine threat to the future of mankind. "There is no denying the crisis that threatens [the family] to its foundations—especially in the Western world," he stated. "When such commitment is repudiated, the key figures of human existence likewise vanish: father, mother, child—essential elements of the experience of being human are lost."

Pope Benedict XVI. "Pope: Address to the Roman Curia." *Vatican News,* December 21, 2012. www.news .va/en/news/pope-address-to-the-roman-curia.

In December 2012 Pope Benedict XVI delivered a stern repudiation of gay marriage as an attack on traditional families and a threat to the future of humankind.

dict the future of the debate over gay marriage or the place of gay people in American society." But he said that he was greatly encouraged by changes in attitude and perception toward gay people over the past several decades. "The opponents of gay equality recognize these changes too. Their campaign to pass a constitutional amendment on marriage stems from their determination to impose the bigotry and inequality of the past on the generations of the future by writing it into the fundamental law of the land. The tide of history is running against them. But nothing in history is inevitable, and none of these changes are irreversible. As always, our future lies in our own hands."[66]

NOTES

Chapter 1: A History of Gay Rights in America

1. Quoted in Donald Webster Cory. *The Homosexual in America: A Subjective Approach.* New York: Arno Press, 1975, p. 270.

2. Quoted in Introduction: *Stonewall Uprising. American Experience.* PBS, 2011. www.pbs.org/wgbh/americanexperience /features/introduction/stonewall-intro.

3. Quoted in *Biography: Stonewall Participants. American Experience.* PBS, 2011. www.pbs.org/wgbh/americanexperience /features/biography/stonewall-participants.

4. Quoted in Roger N. Lancaster. *Sex Panic and the Punitive State.* Berkeley: University of California Press, 2011, p. 42.

5. Quoted in Allen White. "Reagan's AIDS Legacy: Silence Equals Death." *San Francisco Chronicle,* June 8, 2004. www .sfgate.com/opinion/openforum/article/Reagan-s-AIDS-Leg acy-Silence-equals-death-2751030.php#ixzz2IA5ZqSnU.

6. Eric Marcus. *Making Gay History.* New York: HarperPerennial, 2002, p. 245.

7. Larry Kramer. "1,112 and Counting." *New York Native,* March 14–27, 1983. www.indymedia.org.uk/en/2003/05/66 488.html.

8. Supreme Court of the United States. *Lawrence v. Texas* (02-102) 539 U.S. 558 (2003). www.law.cornell.edu/supct/html /02-102.ZS.html.

Chapter 2: Marriage—the Final Frontier in Gay Rights

9. Evan Wolfson. *Why Marriage Matters: America, Equality, and Gay People's Right to Marry.* New York: Simon and Schuster, 2004, p. 71.

10. Eric Marcus. *Making Gay History*. New York: HarperPerennial, 2002, pp. 245–246.

11. George Chauncey. *Why Marriage?* New York: Basic Books, 2004, p. 125.

12. Quoted in Chauncey. *Why Marriage?*, p. 125.

13. Quoted in Dan Savage. *The Commitment: Love, Sex, Marriage, and My Family*. New York: Dutton, 2005, p. 172.

14. Quoted in Chauncey. *Why Marriage?*, pp. 134–135.

15. Quoted in Dean E. Murphy. "Some Democrats Blame One of Their Own." *New York Times*, November 5, 2004. www.nytimes.com/2004/11/05/politics/campaign/05newsom.html?_r=0.

16. Family Research Council. "The Slippery Slope of Same-Sex 'Marriage,'" 2004. www.frc.org/get.cfm?i=bc04c02.

17. George W. Bush. "President Calls for a Constitutional Amendment Protecting Marriage," February 24, 2004. http://georgewbush-whitehouse.archives.gov/news/releases/2004/02/images/20040224-2_d022404-1-515h.html.

18. Barack Obama. "News Conference by the President," December 22, 2010. www.whitehouse.gov/the-press-office/2010/12/22/news-conference-president.

19. Andrew Sullivan. "The First Gay President." *Newsweek*, May 13, 2012. www.thedailybeast.com/newsweek/2012/05/13/andrew-sullivan-on-barack-obama-s-gay-marriage-evolution.html.

Chapter 3: The Case for Gay Marriage

20. Cynthia Nixon. "Our Sweet Triumph." *Newsweek*, July 25, 2011, p. 15.

21. James Fallows. "No One Asked Me, but . . . (Obama on Same-Sex Marriage)." *Atlantic*, May 9, 2012. www.theatlantic.com/politics/archive/2012/05/no-one-asked-me-but-obama-on-same-sex-marriage/256963/.

22. Quoted in Patricia A. Gozemba and Karen Kahn. *Courting Equality: A Documentary History of America's First Legal Same-Sex Marriages*. Boston: Beacon Press, 2007, p. 154.

23. Ta-Nehisi Coates. "Race and Gay Marriage in Perspective." *Atlantic,* August 3, 2010. www.theatlantic.com/national /archive/2010/08/race-and-gay-marriage-in-perspective /60837/.

24. Samuel G. Freedman, "Gay Marriages Open Gate to Social Stability." *USA Today,* August 18, 2003. www.samuel freedman.com/articles/politics/ust08132003.html.

25. E.J. Graff. "Retying the Knot." *Nation,* June 24, 1996. Reprinted in *Same-Sex Marriage: Pro and Con; A Reader.* Rev. ed. Edited by Andrew Sullivan. New York: Vintage, 2004, p. 135.

26. Andrew Sullivan. "What You Do." *New Republic,* March 3, 1996. Reprinted in *Same-Sex Marriage: Pro and Con; A Reader.* Rev. ed. Edited by Andrew Sullivan. New York: Vintage, 2004, p. 83.

27. Michael Leach. "What Gays and Lesbians Are Teaching Us About Marriage: Soul Seeing." *National Catholic Reporter,* May 25, 2012, p. S3a.

28. Zach Wahls. "What Makes a Family." ZachWahls.com. January 31, 2011. www.zachwahls.com/?page_id=273.

29. National Center for Lesbian Rights. *Adoption by Lesbian, Gay, and Bisexual Parents: An Overview of Current Law.* March 2012. www.nclrights.org/site/DocServer/adptn0204 .pdf?docID=1221.

30. Evan Wolfson. "Enough Marriage to Share: A Response to Maggie Gallagher." In *Marriage and Same-Sex Unions: A Debate,* edited by Lynn D. Wardle et al. Westport, CT: Praeger, 2003, p. 25-26.

31. Glenn Greenwald. "Congratulations to Rush Limbaugh on His Fourth Traditional Marriage." *Salon,* June 6, 2010. www.salon.com/2010/06/06/marriage_18/.

32. Howard Moody. "Sacred Rite or Civil Right?" *Nation,* July 5, 2004, p. 28.

33. Andrew Sullivan. *Virtually Normal: An Argument About Homosexuality.* New York: Knopf, 1995, p. 106.

34. Andrew Sullivan. "Why Gay Marriage Is Good for Straight America." *Newsweek,* July 25, 2011, p. 12.

35. Graff. "Retying the Knot," p. 136.

36. Lance Morrow. "Gay Marriage." *Second Drafts of History: Essays.* New York: Basic Books, 2006, p. 136.

Chapter 4: The Case Against Gay Marriage

37. Orson Scott Card. "What Right Is Really at Stake?" *Rhinoceros Times* (Greensboro, NC), May 3, 2004. http://greensboro .rhinotimes.com/hc.e.211703.lasso.

38. David Limbaugh. "Uprooting Our Biblical Foundation." Davidlimbaugh.com, November 21, 2003. www.davidlim baugh.com/112103.htm.

39. Limbaugh. "Uprooting Our Biblical Foundation."

40. William J. Bennett. *The Broken Hearth: Reversing the Moral Collapse of the American Family.* New York: Doubleday, 2001, pp. 112, 115.

41. Maggie Gallagher. "Why Is Gay Marriage an Issue in This Campaign?" *Human Events,* February 17, 2012. www.human events.com/2012/02/17/why-is-gay-marriage-an-issue -in-this-campaign.

42. Sherif Girgis, Robert George, and Ryan T. Anderson. "What Is Marriage?" *Harvard Journal of Law and Public Policy,* Winter 2010, pp. 245–287.

43. Maggie Gallagher. "What Marriage Is For." *Weekly Standard,* August 4, 2003. Reprinted in *Same-Sex Marriage: Pro and Con; A Reader.* Rev. ed. Edited by Andrew Sullivan. New York: Vintage, 2004, p. 270.

44. U.S. Conference of Catholic Bishops (USCCB). "Marriage: Love and Life in the Divine Plan." Pastoral letter, November 17, 2009, p. 31. www.usccb.org/issues-and-action /marriage-and-family/marriage/love-and-life/upload/pasto ral-letter-marriage-love-and-life-in-the-divine-plan.pdf.

45. Tony Perkins. "The Defense of Marriage Act Is Constitutional." *U.S. News and World Report,* March 14, 2011. www .usnews.com/opinion/articles/2011/03/14/the-defense-of -marriage-act-is-constitutional.

46. Gallagher. "What Marriage Is For," p. 266.

47. Mathew D. Staver. *Same-Sex Marriage: Putting Every Household at Risk.* Nashville: Broadman & Holman, 2004, p. 18.

48. Mollie Ziegler Hemingway. "Same Sex, Different Marriage: Many of Those Who Want Marriage Equality Do Not Want Fidelity." *Christianity Today,* May 2010, p. 52.

49. Maggie Gallagher. "The Case Against Same-Sex Marriage." In John Corvino and Maggie Gallagher. *Debating Same-Sex Marriage.* New York: Oxford University Press, 2012, pp. 126, 213.

50. Focus on the Family. "Religious Liberties," 2011. www.focus onthefamily.com/socialissues/defending-your-values /religious-liberties.aspx.

51. Family Research Council. "The Slippery Slope of Same-Sex 'Marriage,'" 2004. www.frc.org/get.cfm?i=bc04c02.

52. Bennett. *The Broken Hearth,* p. 113.

53. Gallagher, "What Marriage Is For," p. 270.

54. James W. Killen. "Same-Sex Marriage Is Not a Civil Right." *Public Justice Report.* Second Quarter, 2004. www .cpjustice.org/stories/storyReader$1178.

55. Robert P. George. "Rick Santorum Is Right." *National Review,* May 27, 2003. www.nationalreview.com/articles/207032 /rick-santorum-right/robert-p-george.

Chapter 5: The Future of Gay Marriage

56. ABCNews.com. "George Will: 'Quite Literally, the Opposition to Gay Marriage Is Dying,'" December 9, 2012. http:// abcnews.go.com/blogs/politics/2012/12/george-will-quite -literally-the-opposition-to-gay-marriage-is-dying/.

57. E.J. Graff. "One Giant Leap for Gay Rights." *American Prospect,* November 7, 2012. http://prospect.org/article/giant- leap-gay-rights.

58. Margaret Talbot. "Wedding Bells." *New Yorker,* May 21, 2012. www.newyorker.com/talk/comment/2012/05/21/120521 taco_talk_talbot.

59. Kate Pickert. "What Choice? Abortion-Rights Activists Won an Epic Victory in *Roe V. Wade.* They've Been Losing Ever Since." *Time,* January 14, 2013, p. 40.

60. Erik Eckholm. "Push Expands for Legalizing Same-Sex Marriage." *New York Times,* November 12, 2012. www.ny

times.com/2012/11/13/us/advocates-of-gay-marriage-extend-their-campaign.html?pagewanted=all.

61. David French. "The Long-Term Future of the Gay Marriage Debate: Stalemate." *The Corner* (blog). *National Review,* May 10, 2012. www.nationalreview.com/corner/299599/long-term-future-gay-marriage-debate-stalemate-david-french.

62. Quoted in Ashley Powers and Matt Stevens. "Prop. 8: Some Gay Rights Activists Nervous About Supreme Court Review." *L.A. Now* (blog). *Los Angeles Times,* December 7, 2012. http://latimesblogs.latimes.com/lanow/2012/12/prop-8-gay-rights-advocates-resigned-to-more-waiting.html.

63. Daniel Fisher. "Supreme Court Unlikely to Deliver Gay-Marriage Mandate." *Forbes,* December 8, 2012. www.forbes.com/sites/danielfisher/2012/12/08/supreme-court-unlikely-to-deliver-gay-marriage-mandate/.

64. Ross Douthat. "More Perfect Unions." *New York Times,* July 3, 2011. www.nytimes.com/2011/07/04/opinion/04douthat.html?_r=0.

65. Maggie Gallagher. "Reply to Corvino." In John Corvino and Maggie Gallagher. *Debating Same-Sex Marriage.* New York: Oxford University Press, 2012, pp. 223–224.

66. George Chauncey. *Why Marriage?* New York: Basic Books, 2004, p. 166.

DISCUSSION QUESTIONS

Chapter 1: A History of Gay Rights in America

1. What stance did the U.S. government take toward homosexuals during the 1940s and 1950s, and how did this position influence wider societal attitudes?

2. Do you think the 1969 Stonewall riot would have had the same influence if it had not taken place during the civil rights era?

3. Discuss the impact of the AIDS crisis on the gay rights movement.

Chapter 2: Marriage—the Final Frontier in Gay Rights

1. Discuss the primary factors that drove gay activists' increased interest in marriage in the 1980s and 1990s.

2. Explain how the Democratic Party's position on gay marriage evolved from the 1990s to today.

3. Examine the differences between same-sex marriage and civil unions, and explain why some people on both sides of the gay marriage issue have seen civil unions as a compromise option worth pursuing.

Chapter 3: The Case for Gay Marriage

1. Review all the reasons for gay marriage provided by supporters and list the three that make the most sense to you. Explain your reasons you chose these three.

2. Which reason to support gay marriage do you find least convincing? Why?

3. Is gay marriage a "hot topic" in the community in which you live? Why or why not?

Chapter 4: The Case Against Gay Marriage

1. Review all the reasons against gay marriage provided by opponents and list the three that make the most sense to you. Explain your reasons for choosing these three.

2. Which reason to oppose gay marriage do you find least convincing? Why?

3. What are the current policies toward gay marriage and civil unions in your state?

Chapter 5: The Future of Gay Marriage

1. What did commentator George Will mean when he said that opposition to gay marriage is "literally" dying in America?

2. Explain the ways in which movies, television shows, and other popular media might influence attitudes toward gay marriage in the years ahead.

3. Based on the available evidence, do you think that gay marriage will become more broadly accepted in the United States over the next thirty years? Why or why not?

ORGANIZATIONS TO CONTACT

Family Research Council (FRC)
801 G St. NW
Washington, DC 20001
phone: (202) 393-2100
website: www.frc.org

Founded in 1983, the FRC describes itself as an organization that is dedicated to advancing faith, family, and freedom in public policy and the culture from a Christian worldview. FRC is one of the country's leading groups opposing same-sex marriage.

Focus on the Family
8605 Explorer Dr.
Colorado Springs, CO 80920
phone: (800) 232-6459
website: www.focusonthefamily.com

This is a conservative Christian organization that promotes traditional family values, including heterosexual marriage. It is a source of a wide range of information delineating arguments against the legalization of same-sex marriage.

Gay and Lesbian Advocates and Defenders (GLAD)
30 Winter St. Suite 800
Boston, MA 02108

GLAD is New England's largest gay advocacy organization. It focuses on providing educational materials and legal resources to "end discrimination based on sexual orientation, HIV status, and gender identity and expression."

Human Rights Campaign (HRC)
1640 Rhode Island Ave. NW
Washington, DC 20036-3278
phone: (800) 777-4723
website: www.hrc.org

Founded in 1980, HRC touts itself as America's largest organization devoted to achieving full civil rights for lesbian, gay, bisexual and transgender Americans. The organization engages in political advocacy and grassroots campaigns with the help of more than 1.5 million members and supporters nationwide.

Lesbian Gay Bisexual & Transgender Project (LGBT Project)
125 Broad St. 18th Floor
New York, NY 10004
phone: (212) 549-2500
website: www.aclu.org/lgbt-rights

The LGBT Project is a special campaign of the American Civil Liberties Union (ACLU). It is dedicated to the establishment of a society in which all people—including LGBT citizens—have full constitutional rights of equality, privacy and personal autonomy, and freedom of expression and association.

National Organization for Marriage (NOM)
2029 K St. NW, Suite 300
Washington, DC 20006
phone: (888) 894-3604
website: www.nationformarriage.org

NOM was founded in 2007 in response to what the organization termed "the growing need for an organized opposition to same-sex marriage in state legislatures." It provides educational materials, political messaging assistance, and other resources to defeat gay marriage initiatives at the federal, state, and local levels.

Books and Articles

David Blankenhorn. "Defining Marriage Down Is No Way to Save It." *Weekly Standard,* April 2, 2007. www.weeklystandard.com/Content/Public/Articles/000/000/013/451noxve.asp. This article argues that giving marriage rights to same-sex couples will cause further strain on traditional heterosexual marriages in America.

George Chauncey. *Why Marriage? The History Shaping Today's Debate over Gay Equality.* New York: Basic Books, 2004. This pro–gay marriage work provides a brisk and understandable overview of the history of the gay civil rights movement in America.

John Corvino and Maggie Gallagher. *Debating Same-Sex Marriage.* New York: Oxford University Press, 2012. This book presents a passionate debate between a dedicated opponent of gay marriage and an equally steadfast supporter of same-sex marriage.

James Dobson. *Marriage Under Fire: Why We Must Win This Battle.* Sisters, OR: Multnomah, 2004. One of America's best-known leaders of the Religious Right explains his unyielding opposition to same-sex marriage.

Maggie Gallagher. "What Marriage Is For: Children Need Mothers and Fathers." *Weekly Standard,* August 4, 2003. www.weeklystandard.com/Content/Public/Articles/000/000/002/939pxiqa.asp. Well-known gay marriage critic Maggie Gallagher sums up her concerns in this well-known article.

Abigail Garner. *Families Like Mine: Children of Gay Parents Tell It Like It Is.* New York: HarperCollins, 2004. This defense of gay marriage and same-sex households collects the stories of boys and girls who grew up with gay parents.

Patricia A. Gozemba and Karen Kahn. *Courting Equality: A Documentary History of America's First Legal Same-Sex Marriages.* Boston: Beacon Press, 2007. This richly illustrated book relates the experiences of some of the first same-sex couples to be legally married in Massachusetts in 2004.

Jonathan Katz. *Lesbians and Gay Men in the U.S.A.: A Documentary History.* New York: Crowell, 1976. This documentary collection guides readers through the history of homosexuality in America from colonial times through the early years of the gay civil rights movement.

Jonathan Rauch. *Gay Marriage: Why It Is Good for Gays, Good for Straights and Good for America.* New York: Times Books/Henry Holt, 2004. A detailed defense of gay marriage and its potentially beneficial influence on American life by a prominent gay journalist and activist

Andrew Sullivan, ed. *Same-Sex Marriage: Pro and Con; A Reader.* Rev. ed. New York: Vintage, 2004. This collection gathers a wide array of pro– and anti–gay marriage perspectives through American history. It is edited by—and includes contributions from—the prominent gay marriage advocate and political commentator Andrew Sullivan.

Websites

Assault on Gay America: The Life and Death of Billy Jack Gaither (www.pbs.org/wgbh/pages/frontline/shows/assault/). This website is the companion to a documentary by the PBS news show *Frontline*. It examines the murder of one gay man in 1999 to cover the wider issue of homophobic violence and antigay attitudes in America.

Gay Marriage and Homosexuality (www.pewforum.org/Topics /Issues/Gay-Marriage-and-Homosexuality/). This website maintained by the Pew Forum on Religion and Public Life provides a wide range of information on the cultural, political, legal, and religious angles of the same-sex marriage debate.

Stonewall Uprising (www.pbs.org/wgbh/americanexperience /films/stonewall/). This website is a companion to *Stonewall Uprising*, a PBS *American Experience* documentary. It includes primary sources, a photo gallery, video, and other information about this pivotal event in American history.

A Visual History of the Gay-Rights Movement (www.time.com /time/photogallery/0,29307,1900959,00.html). This nineteen-piece photo and text gallery from *Time* takes viewers on a historical tour of the gay rights movement in America, beginning with the Stonewall riots and concluding with Barack Obama's endorsement of same-sex marriage.

INDEX

PICTURE CREDITS

Cover: © Lisa F. Young/Shutterstock.com

© AFP/Getty Images, 40

© Akademie/Alamy, 10

© AP Images/George Rizer, 33

© AP Images/J. Scott Applewhite, 73

© AP Images/Phelan M.Ebenhack, 63

© AP Images/Ron Edmondsk, 35

© B Christopher/Alamy, 81

© Boston Globe via Getty Images, 44

© Christophe Simon/AFP/Getty Images, 82

© Gale, Cengage Learning, 15, 32

© Getty Images, 12, 23, 27, 38, 43, 47, 55, 74, 78

© Hulton Archive/Getty Images, 31

© imagebroker/Alamy, 19

© Jennie Hart/Alamy, 67

© MCT via Getty Images, 16

© Novastock/Alamy, 69

© Rod Lankey, Jr./The Washington Times/Landov, 61

© Roll CALL/Getty Images, 58, 64, 76

© Thomas J. Peterson/Alamy, 9

© Time & Life Pictures/Getty Images, 52

© Wire Image/Getty Images, 50

ABOUT THE AUTHOR

Kevin Hillstrom is an independent scholar who has written numerous books on environmental and social issues, U.S. politics and policy, and American history.